MAKE MONEY AS A VIRTUAL ASSISTANT

GAIN FLEXIBILITY AND FREEDOM BY
OFFERING SERVICES ONLINE

GINA HORKEY

CONTENTS

Copyright	iii
Free Bonus	iv
1. Introduction	1
2. Take Inventory of Your Skills	9
3. Choose Your First Service Offering	19
4. Set Your Rates	29
5. Prepare Your Online Presence	38
6. Sourcing Prospects To Pitch	49
7. Send Your First Few Pitches	60
8. Land Your First Client	72
9. Collect Your First Paycheck	82
10. Scale Your Business	93
11. Conclusion	103
Notes	105
About Gina Horkey	106
Excerpt: Make Money As A Freelance Writer	107

Copyright © 2020 by Gina Horkey

All rights reserved. No part of this publication may be reproduced, distributed, or transmitted in any form or by any means, including photocopying, recording, or other electronic or mechanical methods, without the prior written permission of the publisher, except in the case of brief quotations embodied in reviews and certain other non-commercial uses permitted by copyright law.

The information provided within this book is for general informational purposes only. While the authors try to keep the information up-to-date and correct, there are no representations or warranties, express or implied, about the completeness, accuracy, reliability, suitability or availability with respect to the information, products, services, or related graphics contained in this book for any purpose. Any use of this information is at your own risk.

Any advice that is provided in this book is based on the experience of the authors and does not reflect the opinion of the distributor. All opinions expressed in this book are solely the opinion of the authors.

Disclaimer:
Some of the links in this book may be affiliate links. If you click them and decide to buy something, we may be paid a commission. This won't cost you any extra. We only include links to products or services that we either use or would happily use ourselves.

FREE BONUS

As a thank-you for buying this book, I have created some bonus resources to help you on your journey. These resources will help you:

> Understand the skills and qualities you need to be a great virtual assistant

> Identify, price and market your services

> Create a flexible work schedule while providing a sustainable income

Download your bonus resources at:
https://horkeyhandbook.com/book-bonus/

1
INTRODUCTION

As you open the pages of this book, take a quick minute to think about the current state of your life. How's it looking? Are you satisfied? Better yet, do you love how you spend your time and whom you spend it with? Are you living the way you'd always hoped you would?

Because here's the thing – I've been there. I know what it's like when you feel as if your life isn't going the way you hoped it would. You think, *is this really it*? But I'm also a believer that with the right mindset and information you can have the life you want.

How do I know?

Well, I was 16 when I started college.

I was in my junior year of high school. And I knew I'd be responsible for my college tuition. So I decided to take advantage of the state of Minnesota's offer to pay for it.

I grew up in a rural area, and online classes weren't a thing yet. Plus I didn't have a computer or internet access at home. Since the nearest physical location was 45 minutes away, I took a family friend up on her offer of room and board in exchange for a nanny job close to campus.

I had posh digs – an inflatable mattress which I stored in her bedroom during the day and slept on in the living room at night.

In addition to caring for her energetic four-year-old, I took a full course load and worked part-time as a server at a local restaurant. I finished my junior and senior years of high school while also completing my freshman and sophomore years of college, incurring not a cent of student loan debt in the process.

Twelve years later, I had two beautiful babies, a wonderful husband, and a flexible career in personal finance that paid all of the bills. On paper, I had nothing to be miserable about.

But it wasn't fulfilling. I wasn't passionate about what I was doing, and at 29 I wasn't ready to settle for good enough.

I was desperate for change but oh so afraid. I knew that finance wasn't what I wanted to be doing. But I continued to force that square peg into the circle slot for a few more years.

Can You Relate?

So there I found myself on tax day in 2014 searching for something different. I started with Google, which led me to the world of freelance writing. Within a couple of months, I had launched a website and got busy pitching my writing services to prospective clients.

I worked at my new biz in the early morning hours before heading off to my day job. I had some good success with freelance writing. HorkeyHandBook.com started simply as a place to showcase my writing samples. But I also knew that I wanted to take my freelance business full-time and leave my day job behind.

As the breadwinner for my family of four, I knew that I'd need a consistent and predictable income. Since I had experience with in-person support, I figured Virtual Assistance (VA) work couldn't be that much of a leap. And I knew I'd be good at it.

So I started doing a little research on what a VA did, how to get paid, and so on. Then, I ran across someone who could really use my services.

I asked him to hire me. And he said yes.

Within four months of starting my business I was making $4,000 on the side. Within eight months I said so long to my 9-5, for good. I proved again that with a little bit of focus and the right motivation, big things are possible.

Now that you've heard my story, let me ask you: if your life was exactly how you wanted it to be, what would it look like? How would you spend your time? Where would you spend it? What would your finances look like, and what life goals would you have achieved?

What could you achieve that you never thought was possible?

If you're reading this book, you must have some idea that offering services online as a Virtual Assistant could be the vehicle to making your dream a reality. Do you want to spend more time with your family and kids? Be in control of how you spend your time? Have unlimited income potential? Open doors to opportunities you may not even know exist yet?

Because here's the reality – a Virtual Assistant is someone who:

- Gets paid to offer services from home (or anywhere they want to)
- Chooses exactly what kind of work they want to do and with whom they want to work
- Decides when they want to work, including how often and for how long
- Has unlimited opportunities for specializing in lucrative and in-demand services
- Determines their market rate and their destiny!

In my own experience as well as that of the thousands of students I've taught, being a VA is the best way to get started online and open doors. It's an incredible way to get paid while you learn the "online marketing game." Then, apply those skills to whatever business idea or opportunity you may want to explore in the future. It's the gateway to entrepreneurialism, if you want it to be. And in today's online world, that means unlimited potential.

Since 2014, I worked with three main recurring VA clients at a higher-than-average rate, which allowed me to pay the bills at home. And I wasn't working full-time, either. I also launched my first digital product that year. Since then, I've continued to add courses and products every year.

It wasn't until 2019 that I stopped offering services to clients and transitioned into a full-time entrepreneur. It was hard to part ways with my last client. I was making a very good wage on very part-time hours. He even flew me to Prague to take part in a team retreat!

I've worked from my home in central Minnesota, the condo we rent in South Padre Island, Texas, all over the lovely state of Alaska, during road trips to places like Yellowstone, and even overseas! It's truly amazing where my VA biz has taken me.

Something for Everyone

So if being a VA holds so much opportunity, why doesn't everyone do it?

Well to start with, a lot of us have been conditioned that a traditional job equals security and stability. Freelancing is often associated with unpredictable or variable income.

But as I write this book, over half of the US workforce is currently unemployed. Sadly, many people are experiencing the harsh reality that traditional employment doesn't guarantee stability.

Virtual Assistant income, on the other hand, can be predictable and dependable – both in the hours that you work and the pay that you receive. You have control over this based on what services and packages you decide to offer to clients and whom you choose to work with.

For example, I used to offer a monthly retainer to my clients for email management services. It didn't matter how many hours I worked or when I did the work – I still earned the same pay month in, month out. And we all know that it's easier to budget for expenses when you know what your income will be.

I enjoyed the security of my VA income immensely as I moved away from my full-time job and transitioned to working online full-time towards the end of 2014. As the sole income earner, it's been huge for my family's peace of mind.

And the journey that started with my freelance writing side hustle is about to take yet another amazing turn that I never would have expected. In the coming year, I'll be a college professor at Lakewood University teaching folks just like you how to become Virtual Assistants. It just goes to show you never know where this journey could take you.

The story I just shared with you is *my* story. I've seen people go about this in lots of different ways. And while there are steps to take and best practices, when it comes to building a business, there's no one blueprint you must follow. You get to do this on your terms, in the way that works for you and your family, at your pace.

So for you, that may mean picking up a client or two, finding or making time in your schedule to work on your business, and then scaling up until you can ditch that 9-5 like I did. Or it might mean creating a side hustle of one to two clients and being happy with that forever.

The bottom line is that when you want something bad enough, you have to get creative. Things really do have a way of coming together when you set your mind on something you truly want, then go after it until you get it.

Since 2015, I've helped thousands and thousands of people just like you realize their dreams of starting a successful Virtual Assistant business working from wherever they want. My favorite emails are the ones saying they've landed their first client or just given their notice at their day job.

Celebrating others' success lights me up inside.

And if I can do it, I know you can too.

Why You've Made the Best Decision To Become a VA

Hopefully you can see how building a service-based business as a VA can impact your life. But you still may be wondering, *Is there enough work out there?*

The short answer is – yes! Freelancing is growing at a rapid rate worldwide, and more and more business owners are contracting out for services. They save a significant amount of money on taxes and employment costs, and thankfully, the era of paying someone to sit at a desk all day is falling by the wayside. On average, a business owner can save up to $11,000 per employee every year just by outsourcing to contractors.[1]

And the reality is that in our digital age the majority of work doesn't need to be done in person. Most tasks can be handled remotely, including meeting face-to-face. A survey conducted by Upwork and the Freelancers Union found that freelancers make up more than 35% of the workforce in the US as of 2019. And the number of freelancers domestically has been on a steady rise (8.1% over the last four years). If this trend continues, it's predicted that 50% of our workforce will be working from home in 10 years.[2]

Your First Steps To Becoming a VA

A huge benefit of VA work is that with the right information and mindset, anyone can do it. You don't need a special degree (or any degree at all) or even specific experience offering services. Everyone has some kind of skill they can turn into a service to offer and get paid for.

In the following chapters, I'm going to systematically walk you through nine steps to get started as a Virtual Assistant. If you implement what you read, including the action steps at the end of each chapter, you'll have everything you need to get your VA business off the ground by the time you finish this book.

Here are the steps:

1. Take inventory of your skills
2. Choose your first service offering
3. Set your rates
4. Prepare your online presence
5. Source prospects to pitch
6. Send your first few pitches
7. Land your first client
8. Collect your first paycheck
9. Scale your business

How do I know these are the steps to making things happen as a VA as quickly as possible? As I mentioned earlier, I've helped thousands and thousands of people get started. But don't take my word for it. Here's what some of my #FullyBookedVASystem[3] students have said:

Well I did it. I signed a substantial contract allowing me to give notice for my full-time job. Two weeks and I'll be a full-time Virtual Assistant making more than I make now as a full-time employee!!!! ~Jeannette C.

... I just worked my first three hours managing a client's emails... I got hired after my first actual pitch and it's beyond any of the goals I had set for myself when I started this three weeks ago. ~Fareeha F.

I'm seriously freaking out right now! I've only been pitching for six days!!! And I just got my first client – we're starting a trial period in two days. If this works out, this is seriously a dream client for me. So excited and grateful. ~Arishonne S.

I woke up this morning with my third client confirmed in my inbox. This is a big win because I told myself that when I got the third, it's time to quit my 9-5! I'm now that much closer to being a stay-at-home dog-mom... This client came from talking to a friend of a friend at a party whose boss just happened to be focusing on scaling up his business. ~Jacqueline B.

From brand new beginners to VAs scaling their businesses, there is something for everybody. Do you see the potential here for you?

Your Next Few Weeks

By now you should be very excited about the decision you've made. Here's what's next for you.

Read the following chapters and take immediate action on what you're reading – especially the action steps at the end of each chapter. Don't forget to download your companion workbook here:

https://horkeyhandbook.com/book-bonus/

It doesn't need to take you long to read this book. But if you follow these steps, you can land your first client in the next few weeks or less.

I've laid out a systematic approach that I've seen work thousands of times before. I've made the steps as easy and seamless as possible for you to get up and running as a Virtual Assistant quickly. And from there, the sky's the limit when it comes to what this amazing online adventure has in store for you!

Remember that you *can* do this. I'm here to cheer you on every step of the way and can't wait to hear about your success.

So enjoy the following chapters and get excited about the incredible decision you've made to become a Virtual Assistant!

2

TAKE INVENTORY OF YOUR SKILLS

So what do you think? Do you have what it takes to become a VA? With the right motivation, focus, and information, the short answer is absolutely yes!

Two common questions that come up for a lot of people considering putting themselves out there offering services virtually are whether they have anything to offer the marketplace and whether they can really do this or not.

In other words, what exactly do you need to be a good Virtual Assistant who makes a decent living online?

The longer answer to this comes in two parts:

1. The personality traits that make you a great VA
2. Existing skill sets that can be translated into services

In this chapter we'll take a look at the kinds of traits I've consistently seen in successful VAs and how to take inventory of your existing skills. Lastly – but super important – we'll discuss how to set realistic goals.

Traits That Make You an Excellent VA

When thinking about what kinds of traits a business owner might be looking for in a VA, the best place to start is exactly right there – in the shoes of a business owner.

As I'm sure you'll learn when you build your service offerings online, your new business becomes your baby in a way, meaning, most successful business owners pour their hearts and souls into creating a business from the ground up. They spend time, effort, and passion turning their vision into a reality.

It stands to reason that if someone is entrusting the ins and outs of their business to you, they would want to have confidence in your skills and characteristics.

And when it comes to desirable personality traits, there's also the nature of the work to consider.

As a Virtual Assistant, you're working from home (or wherever you want), ideally during hours that suit you, and with an expectation that you'll be delivering your services in a timely, efficient, and quality manner.

The very nature of that kind of work calls for a disciplined, take-charge, "go-getter" kind of attitude!

You're also entering into the world of online business. Even if you're working with brick-and-mortar companies, the majority of business tasks are handled online, via apps, computer software, etc. There are a ton of ways to get things done these days. And businesses are unique in the tools and resources they use.

So no matter what service you're offering, you must embrace this fact and be open, willing, and eager to learn new things.

The majority of business owners are happy to train you to use the systems and tools they have in place. They don't always expect that someone will know how to do the things they're looking for in the exact way they'd like them done. And when new tools become available they're also happy to pay someone else to figure out how to implement them.

This is part of the fun as a VA – being paid to learn! As you learn new things, not only does the process become easier, but you also build a toolbox of marketable skills to bring to other potential clients.

A great Virtual Assistant is someone who:

1. **Is organized** – Having an organized approach to your work will serve you in your business and will show in the quality of work you deliver to your clients.
2. **Is reliable** – Showing up and doing what you've said you'll do is vital to every business owner. There's a big trust factor, and reliability rates highly, if not at the top, of desirable traits.
3. **Has a positive attitude** – You're essentially joining a business owner in their vision. Having a positive, can-do attitude makes you a great teammate.
4. **Takes initiative** – Someone who knows when to take charge and get things done without needing to be micromanaged. While it's a fine balance between knowing when to ask questions and just handling things, most business owners want to trust that their VA will get things done without constant supervision.
5. **Communicates well** – Clear, professional communication skills are something that should be established from the very first point of contact with a client. Being able to communicate in a clear and efficient way is a highly-valued trait.
6. **Is open to learning new things** – An eagerness to learn is vital and can also open doors to new opportunities. Showing someone you're excited to learn increases the chances that you'll be given more tasks to do. And of course, more tasks equal more pay.

While some people naturally possess some (or even all) of these traits, others can be learned or developed. Keep in mind that most business owners are clear about what kinds of traits they're looking for in a VA. This makes it easy for you to decide whether or not you'll be a good fit for each other.

List Your Existing Skills

The second part of evaluating what you bring to the table as a Virtual Assistant is taking a look at your existing skills. A common belief is that to be successful as a VA, you need to have a hard, marketable skill.

In fact, the fear that you don't know what kind of service you'll offer can unfortunately keep you from moving forward and pursuing VA work to its fullest potential.

But here's the truth: everyone has some kind of experience or skill that can be repositioned into a service offering. You just may not realize what it is yet!

For example, with my experience working for Jenny Craig, later in personal finance, and even as a waitress, I have a background with in-person support and customer service. Translating those into skills I could offer as a VA wasn't too difficult.

You don't have to be limited by what you can do right now, either. Down the line in your business, you may end up offering services that have nothing to do with what you currently know how to do. Maybe there's something out there that's always interested you, or that you don't even know about yet.

As you begin doing VA work, a fun part of the process is discovering new avenues and opportunities and deciding exactly what kind of work you want (and love) to do. Keep in mind that you're crafting a business on your terms. It can look however you want it to.

Take Kathi, for example. She's a past student who spent 13 years as a registered nurse. Even though she was passionate about helping people, she was completely burned out in the nursing field. Kathi took her interest and expertise in nutritional therapy, made a leap of faith, and started her own business supporting other practitioners as a VA.

In a Facebook group for nutritional therapists, Kathi asked, "Has anyone here worked with a VA before?" Within 10 minutes of that post, she landed her first client. Ten months into her journey, Kathi was making almost as much as she was in her full-time nursing career.

Do you see the potential for turning your skills into a business you love?

Right now, our goal is to go for the quick win: to get you set up and offering a service you can do right away, so you can become profitable as soon as possible.

We'll explore this further in the next chapter, including how to translate your background and skills into services and choose service offerings. For now, let's start with taking inventory of your existing skills.

Taking Inventory

In some cases, figuring out your existing skill set will be obvious. For example, someone with admin experience in an office setting will have clear skills they can identify, like organization and verbal and written communication skills.

In other cases, existing skills may not be clear, especially if you've been out of work for a while. And it might be difficult to make a connection between past or current experiences and hard skills.

If that's you, here are some questions to get you thinking about what skills you already have:

1. What Is Your Work Experience?

What kinds of tasks have you performed for pay? Again, some of the skills you've used in previous work settings may be obvious, but there could also be others you're not thinking of.

For example, if you've worked in a restaurant setting, you would likely be good at thinking on your feet, customer service, and perhaps even project management, depending on your role.

2. What Are You Good At?

Aside from tasks you may have performed for previous jobs, are there things you're naturally good at? Think about things that other people have complimented you on.

For example, do you have a really awesome personal social media presence? Do you keep your emails organized and your inbox cleared out? Then you've likely got some social media or email management skills.

Tori, also a past student, received compliments on how "pretty" her personal Instagram profile was on a regular basis. That feedback got Tori's wheels turning, so she pursued some more in-depth social media training. She's since built a successful business offering social media services to business owners.

3. What Are You Passionate About?

Think about the things that are most important to you, that you love to do. Are there any skills you can uncover there?

Have you organized any groups at your church or kids' school? Done any writing about a topic you care deeply about, perhaps a letter to the editor or your local congressman? Think team management or content creation, for example.

Sierra, another past student of mine, always had an interest in travel. So she started her own travel blog to educate herself on the ins and outs of blogging and began offering her services to other travel bloggers. She runs a successful part-time business from wherever she happens to be traveling, in an area of interest she absolutely loves.

4. What Are Your Past Experiences?

What kinds of things have you done in the past that required specific knowledge or expertise, including hobbies?

Maybe you've been a volunteer or part of a service club or organization, such as the treasurer or fundraiser? You may also have some unique interests or hobbies that involve a specific skill or knowledge. Think about the different roles you've had and what was involved. There are most likely some hard skills that go along with those.

Taking inventory of your existing skills is really an opportunity to get creative – and get excited. Why? Because the process gets your wheels turning about the possibilities of crafting a business doing something you enjoy, something you're already good at. Because let's face it, we're all more motivated to show up every day for something we love to do and know we can do well.

A Word About Digital Skills

Another common misconception is that you need to have advanced digital skills. But don't let this stop you. If the digital world isn't a part of your previous experience, that definitely doesn't count you out as a great VA.

We've already covered that the nature of the job is working online and using tools, apps, and software. But it's not complicated. The basic tools you need to get started are:

- A computer
- An understanding of how to navigate the internet
- A reliable internet connection
- A way to communicate with clients – email and ideally a video chat platform like Skype or Zoom

With so many resources at your fingertips on the internet, such as Google searches or YouTube videos, you can figure out just about anything these days. That's where your "willingness to learn" trait will really serve you as a VA.

Setting Realistic Goals

The next step in creating a solid foundation for your new business is setting realistic goals. I really can't say enough about how important this is! When you're clear about where you want to go and what you want to accomplish, you're far more likely to get there.

You might already have some ideas about why starting your own business as a VA is a good fit for you and what you'd like to accomplish.

For example, you may be looking for:

- Uncapped income
- Time flexibility and freedom
- The ability to be there for your children
- The option to leave your 9-5 job

My goal is for you to land your first client as you finish taking action on this book. But where do you want to be in the next year? How about in the next three and five years?

Make some time to really think about this question. Be aware that the decisions you make today and the actions you take will bring you closer to these goals when you stay consistent, diligent, and focused.

Also keep in mind that building any business is more of a marathon than a sprint. The consistent actions you take now will have a snowball effect. And even when it doesn't seem to matter in the moment or have an immediate outcome, it all adds up. Small actions equal big results.

Now that you've given some thought as to where you'd like to see yourself – and your business – the next step is to streamline those goals.

Take your vision for your future and create goals that are S.M.A.R.T.: specific, measurable, actionable, results-oriented, and time-sensitive.

For example, take a goal like "stay home with my kids," and put it into more focused, actionable language, like this:

Create $3,000 per month in income from my Virtual Assistant business within six months. Increase this income to $5,000 per month and put in my notice at my current employer within the next 12 months.

I also encourage you to come up with a "Dream Big" goal. Maybe it's an overseas traveling adventure, buying a first (or second) home, or fulfilling a dream that's been on your heart for a long time.

It should be something that gets you excited, but also makes you a little nervous! Why? Well as the saying goes, if your dreams don't make you a little nervous, they're not big enough!

This goal may not be your primary focus as you move forward in your business. But you can tuck it away, knowing that the only people who fail at achieving them are the ones who quit. I firmly believe that success as a VA is available to almost everyone.

Don't believe me? We've had students on the autism spectrum, residents all over the world, people caring for special needs children or aging parents, and tons of moms that are actively growing a business while raising young kids. All of them have succeeded at working online.

Action Steps

1. Take a few minutes and review the six traits to see how you fare. Do you feel you have the traits of a great VA? Are there some you need to work on?
2. Set a timer for 15 minutes and write down three to five skills you currently have. Remember to think through the previous jobs and responsibilities you've had so far. If you get stuck,

you could ask a close friend or family member what they think you're good at.
3. Take a minute to envision where you'd like to be in the next year, three years and five years. If this intimidates you, feel free to focus on shorter timelines like 30, 90, and 180 days.

* * *

By now I hope you're excited about the opportunity that exists for you as a VA. You're doing exactly the right thing in gathering information and putting the pieces together so that you can take the next steps toward your success.

While this is a business that anyone can succeed in, it's helpful to be aware of what kinds of traits will give you an edge for success. And none of them are especially difficult, out of the ordinary, or unachievable if they're not something that comes naturally to you.

Now that you're armed with the right information, you can cultivate the traits that will help you stand out and build great relationships with clients.

I can't emphasize enough that almost everyone has a skill that they can turn into a service. For you, it may be straightforward. Or perhaps there may need to be some creativity involved. But there are millions of businesses out there with all kinds of needs. There really is something for everyone when it comes to VA work.

Lastly, your goals are your guidepost. Setting goals will not only give you focus, but it will remind you why you're doing what you're doing in the first place. I recommend keeping your new goals somewhere you can see them and revisiting them often to stay on track. Use these as another opportunity to be very excited about the potential of your business and future!

In the next chapter, we'll explore how to translate your existing skills into services and look at what kinds of opportunities are out there.

3

CHOOSE YOUR FIRST SERVICE OFFERING

As we move forward adding layers to your journey, you'll see that with each layer of information, things get more exciting.

So far, we've seen the opportunity that exists in the marketplace with millions of businesses outsourcing for services. And that everyone has some kind of skill that can be turned into a marketable service. That means there's a place for *you*.

Our next step is to narrow down what service you can offer right off the bat as you look for your first client. For many VAs starting out, this is where it starts to become real.

Before we get into narrowing down your services, it's worth taking a minute to think about the most helpful approach to this. While our aim is to get you hired and providing services as quickly as possible, you are also in the beginning stages of building a long-term, sustainable, and successful business.

Therefore, I want to provide you with some context so you can see the bigger picture.

Why Is It Important To Choose a Primary Service Offering?

You might be wondering why it's so important to figure out what service you can offer right away. Why not just put yourself out there and see what people are looking for? Maybe start looking through job boards and see what opportunities are there?

Well, the first reason is that our goal is to get you set up and working with a client within a few weeks. If you have focus regarding what service you're offering, your chances of finding someone to hire you go way up.

Knowing what service you'll offer also gives you credibility and legitimizes you as a VA. Think back to the last chapter when you put yourself in the mindset of a business owner. Being able to confidently communicate what it is you can do for a business increases your odds of being trusted – and hired.

Don't Be a Jack (or Jill) of All Trades

It's tempting for new VAs to want to get out there and offer anything to anyone in the hopes of landing work quickly. While this mindset is totally understandable, especially if you need income fast, it's really not productive long-term.

In fact, taking this approach can turn out to be discouraging. It translates into a lack of focus and typically results in you being all over the place. Consequently, it can really slow your progress down.

Remember that saying, "Jack of all trades, master of none"?

Business owners who are looking to fill a need and pay well for it are seeking someone who knows what they're doing. Of course, there are businesses out there looking to hire "worker bees" who will do anything that's needed. But they typically don't pay well, and often the work isn't rewarding.

While it's okay to head into your journey being open to trying new services and tasks, I don't recommend starting there for the reasons I've just covered.

Your mindset as you're starting out should be:

- Short Term: Pick a service, get hired, and create income quickly.
- Long(er) Term: Narrow down the services you enjoy offering and build a sustainable business around them.

My friend and collaborator, Hailey Thomas, got the ball rolling in her VA business by offering general admin services. Why? Because with her corporate background, she was confident she could get started offering this kind of service right away to get her business up and running.

Hailey also wasn't completely sure what business owners were looking for. She just needed to get her business started and earn an income as soon as possible.

As time went on, Hailey's business evolved to project management, human resources support, and inbox/document management. But she didn't stop there.

Hailey has continued to evolve her business, and it's working out really well for her. Aside from creating two online courses and launching a couple of podcasts, Hailey is now a mindset coach for online entrepreneurs.

So as you can see from Hailey's story, when it comes to choosing a service, you just need to pick one and get started! Your business can evolve as much or as little as you want. It's really up to you and your goals, which brings me to my next point...

You Can't Choose Wrong

Choosing a service to get started with is where a lot of new VAs have trouble. They tend to overthink things and get stuck in analysis paralysis.

The great news is that you really can't choose wrong when it comes to picking your first service. It's not set in stone, and the worst-case scenario is that you find that something doesn't resonate with you, or no one is looking to hire for it. You can always shift gears and change directions.

Remember, you are in the best position to craft a business doing what you love, when you want to do it, and with whom you want to work. And as you move forward working with clients, you'll find that you have more flexibility in choosing the work you want to do.

A Word About the Bigger Picture

Whether it's a service you stick with or end up moving on from, your service offering will ultimately give you direction regarding something you can specialize in when you have more experience.

Again, it's okay to keep an open mind about what you want to do in the beginning stages. But in the long term, I always recommend narrowing down on one or more services and becoming really skilled at those.

Why? Because specialists are in higher demand. They're taken more seriously in the marketplace and perhaps most significantly, they make more money!

It may end up being the service you choose today, or it may be something entirely different down the road. Whatever you settle on, dig in and become really good at it by pursuing some advanced education or training. It will definitely be worth it.

Choosing a Service To Start With

In the last chapter, we took inventory of the current skills you have. Review the list of three to five skills you created. Keep it in the back of your mind as we take a look at some of the main categories of services. Think about what you can bring to the table and where those skills might fit best.

As you read through, notice what stands out to you. It could be an area that's familiar to you. Or perhaps something you don't have direct experience in, but you want to learn how to do. If it's the latter, be sure to pick something that you're confident you could do successfully as you'll be offering it as a marketable service.

And don't forget that it's okay to be creative when it comes to making a connection between your skills and a service.

As we go through these categories, also keep in mind that there is a plethora of ways you can provide services online. These are just some of the primary areas to focus on when you're narrowing down a place to get started quickly.

Are you ready?

Administrative

This is a broad category that covers a lot of ground, but that a lot of businesses need help with. Administrative services can be a great way to get started with a business by handling various admin tasks and then expanding into a position with more duties. This can include more specialized tasks as trust and credibility are established.

I've seen lots of VAs in our private Facebook community build successful long-term client relationships this way. We post client leads looking to hire VAs there almost daily. Oftentimes, they're looking for help with admin tasks and are open to hiring newer, less experienced VAs. As these businesses find someone they trust with entry-level tasks and whom they enjoy working with, these relationships can evolve to include more in-depth duties and higher pay.

How would you know that administrative services might be the offering for you?

If you're highly organized, both physically and digitally, and are energized by the inner workings that keep a business moving and flowing, administrative services might be a great fit.

Tasks involved with this area of service could include email management, working with documents, spreadsheets, and scheduling – basically, those things that business owners want to hand off so they can focus on growing their business.

Administrative services are not to be confused with "busy work." A good admin VA, trusted with their inner workings and processes, can be the lifeblood of a successful business.

Creative

This category of services is definitely for a certain personality type – typically right-brain thinkers. Someone interested in this service area might be excited about coming up with and implementing new ideas. And a good brainstorming session would really get their juices flowing.

Creating content such as blog posts, website copy, and/or email copy falls under this category. And creative service providers typically have great written communication skills. Other areas may include graphic design, social media management, and business branding.

Technical

The technical services area is one that people either love or hate. While all VAs must have some comfort level with the world of technology, offering services in this category is an entirely different beast.

Our team member Daryn Collier is a very talented writer. He's also highly skilled on the tech side. He keeps things moving on the back end of my websites, which is foundational to my business.

After several years working on my online business, it's safe to say that I know some things (a lot of things, actually) about technical stuff. I do enjoy learning about new tools and ways to get things done more easily and efficiently.

But I don't love the technical side of running a business. So having someone like Daryn, who is into tech and great at it, is instrumental to my success in business.

Do you get jazzed about creating and/or maintaining websites, or love tools and software? Do you enjoy learning how to use them, troubleshooting problems, and building automations? Then the world of technical services may be your calling, too.

Support and Sales

This is a great service category for someone who's people-oriented and energized by supporting others. And supporting others can come in a lot of contexts. It can include customer service or providing an excellent user experience for your client's customers. It could be moderating a social media community or even offering products or services through sales.

People who resonate with this service have great verbal communication skills and are not put off by the variety of issues that can come up when dealing with the public. They're good at thinking on their feet and tend to have a personable, professional nature.

One of the VAs on my team, Davi, manages the customer support for my business, including various brands underneath it. I still interact directly with students and my audience because I enjoy it, but Davi manages the majority of support emails that come in.

I get to meet with Davi via video chat on a regular basis, and I'm always reminded why she's so great at her job. She has an awesome, upbeat attitude. Plus she's able to see the humor in almost any situation and talks to people in a professional, personable, and kind way.

Making sure my customers and students have an excellent experience is really important to me. In fact, it's one of the most important aspects of my business! Because of her great energy, contagious upbeat attitude, and professional communication skills, I feel completely confident about Davi being the "voice" of my support team.

Management

This category is for those who don't shrink at communicating clearly with others, managing moving parts, and taking charge. These people tend to be the go-tos for overseeing projects and are very detail-oriented. They understand the dynamics of managing others and how to do so gracefully and professionally.

People who are drawn to management services are excited about getting things done as smoothly and efficiently as possible. They can step back and conceptualize the big picture of what needs to happen to accomplish a goal or complete a project. Services that would fall into this category would be things like project and team management.

Now You Choose

As you read through the five categories of services, which of those stand out to you? Which one sounds like a great fit for you and an area that you could pursue further? Importantly, which category excites you?

Remember, whatever you choose to get started with as a service isn't your final choice, but it should be something that interests you and gets you excited. If you pick something that you're not thrilled about, it will ultimately come out in the quality of your work. And of course, there's that very important factor of building a business doing something you love!

These are broad categories but are also a good place to start narrowing things down. Next, take a look at 150+ Services You Can Offer as a Virtual Assistant (and get paid for!).[1]

Set aside some time and read through the services on this list. Print it and cross out the things that don't sound interesting to you, that you don't know anything about, or that you don't see yourself being passionate about.

Then, go back and highlight the services that do sound interesting, intriguing, and exciting. And since we want to get you in profit as quickly as possible, go back through the list and narrow it down to something you could go and do right now.

Don't get overwhelmed as you go through this list. You may come across things that you didn't even know were marketable services. And hopefully you'll become even more inspired about the potential that's there for you as a VA.

If you can't find a service that you're energized about but do know how to do, go with that for now. Use it as a place to get started. Then, keep your radar up for a service that you can really get into.

Action Steps

1. Read through the 150+ Services pdf.[2]
2. Choose one to two services that you currently know how to do that you can offer to prospective clients.
3. Locate another two to three services that you are interested in learning more about.

* * *

Things are coming together in this adventure you've started out on. We've covered repurposing your skills and translating them into a service you can offer businesses. And you now have a comprehensive list to get your creative juices flowing around what service you can get started offering right away.

Keep in mind that having this service clarified will help you talk with potential clients and increase your chances of getting hired. You'll be able to match what you're offering to what they're looking for and speak confidently about what you can do for their business. Doing so establishes trust and a belief that you'll show up and do it.

Next up, we'll explore the burning question on your mind: what to charge for your services.

4
SET YOUR RATES

Now that we've figured out what your skills are and what service you'll be offering, it's time to talk about getting paid.

Just like choosing a service to offer, when you start figuring out the income potential of your business, things start to feel a lot more real. By now, you should be seeing the potential of this opportunity at an even greater level.

Speaking of potential, we've talked about the demand in the marketplace for VAs and what starting a business like this can do for your life and circumstances. But what we haven't talked about yet is the financial potential – the dollars and cents of this opportunity.

So how much can a VA make?

The Going Rates for Virtual Assistant Services

This can be a difficult answer to nail down as the research out there can be confusing. And even though we're generally doing business on a global level, rates are still impacted by region. More significantly though, VA rates are affected by the level of a VA's experience and specialization.

Reported rates for VAs are also impacted by whether these numbers are coming from people in business for themselves or the large number who choose to work through agencies. There's nothing wrong with sourcing work from agencies or marketplaces like Upwork. But the opportunities on sites like these pay much less than the rates someone in business for themselves could command because the agency or marketplace is taking a cut.

To give you an idea of the reported rates, in 2020 ZipRecruiter reported that the average yearly income for a VA is around $67,000. They also reported an hourly rate ranging from $7.21 to $62.74 with an average of $32 per hour. As you can see, it's a pretty wide range.

In my experience, North American VAs are charging anywhere from $15 to $100 per hour. In our VA Leads Community, we let business owners know that our VAs charge anywhere from $20 to $40 per hour. We won't post any leads looking to pay less than $20 per hour, and I never recommend accepting anything less than this. The average seems to be around $30 to $35 per hour.

Personally, I started at $35 per hour when charging hourly and worked my way up to earning more than $100 an hour before hanging up client work for good in 2019. When I was earning the big bucks, I was no longer charging hourly and had become very efficient at what I did.

What you charge is ultimately up to you, what your income needs are, and of course what's realistic when it comes to getting hired. Later we'll explore the kinds of things you should factor in to figure out your starting rate that will make this journey worth it to you and give you a realistic place to get started.

As we head into this discussion, know that your rates are not set in stone. And as you gain experience and hone your skills, they should increase with each new client you take on. This is just the beginning.

Hourly Rates Versus Retainers

So far we've been discussing VA rates in the context of hourly pay. Why? Because when you're just starting out and are getting a feel for what it looks like, how long things will take, and the effort involved, it makes the most sense to charge hourly.

Charging an hourly rate in the beginning is also easier for you and the client. It's likely that neither of you will know exactly how long the tasks will take. If you try and jump out there right away with a retainer rate (a flat, fixed amount usually charged on a schedule), you run the risk of not earning what you're worth. You may find out that the services you agreed on with your new client are going to be more involved than you thought.

Also, a lot of clients aren't sure how much they should pay for VA services. Until you're more experienced, there's typically a settling-in period with a new client. You're both figuring out how you can meet their needs within their budget and what's reasonable and realistic regarding time expectations.

Some clients are pretty clear on what they need and how long it will take. Other clients can be way out there with their expectations and have a laundry list of tasks to be done in five hours per week. So for that reason, it's helpful to both of you to start with an hourly rate.

That said, it's almost always ideal to move towards a retainer rate in the long term. There are a few reasons for this. First, as you become more efficient with the tasks you're doing for your client, they'll take less time. So in essence, if you're charging an hourly rate, you can get penalized for doing your work more efficiently.

If you're handling tasks efficiently and effectively, there's nothing wrong with asking for a flat fee once you have a handle on how much time those tasks generally take. I'm a big fan of working smarter, not harder.

Another reason it's beneficial to move to a retainer rate is that tracking your time can be a drag after a while. Ideally, you'll establish trust in your working relationships. And your clients will have no problem paying you a set fee each month knowing that you'll get the work done, both well and on time.

And lastly, it will be easier for your client to have a set expense and great for you to know the income you can count on every month. It's a win-win for both of you.

Some VAs stick with the model of starting out with new clients charging an hourly rate, then moving to a retainer rate after a period of time or once the scope of the work is clarified. Other VAs charge solely on a retainer basis once they have a firm grasp on their services, the typical time involved, and the level of income they want to make.

What's important to remember here is that how you set up your business is ultimately up to you. And you can get creative with this.

My friend Mara offers new clients a baseline rate of $45 per hour. She has special project rates and packages that she provides once she's figured out what her client's needs and budget are.

Sierra, on the other hand, has built her business around providing Pinterest management services. She offers three different packages based on whether the client is with or without an existing Pinterest presence and what their ongoing needs are. In Sierra's case, packages make the most sense based on her primary service. She doesn't mention an hourly rate on her services page.

And then you have my friend Mallory. She starts new clients off on a three-month trial period with a discounted rate of $40 per hour. She then offers the option of remaining at an hourly rate (higher than $40 per hour) or transitioning to a monthly membership (retainer) based on a 12-, 16-, or 20-hour-per-week time commitment.

And lastly, remember my friend Hailey? She doesn't even mention hourly rates or packages on her website because of the caliber of clientele she's serving and the high-level offering. Instead, she offers a free "virtual coffee chat" to potential clients to explore their needs and then proposes her fee once she's gathered enough information to quote her rates appropriately.

As you get comfortable with your business, you'll settle on a model that works for you. For now, focus on getting started with that hourly rate and know that it's only the beginning of your earning potential.

Transitioning To a Retainer

If charging a retainer rate is more ideal, how do you transition from an hourly rate to a flat fee? There are a few ways to go about having this discussion with a client:

1. When more tasks are added – your client is clearly happy with the way things are going, so it's a great opportunity to discuss a new rate and method of being paid.
2. At milestone points in time – after two to three months of working together, six months, or even after a few weeks when you've got a handle on the work/time put in.
3. Build into an initial agreement with a client (we'll cover contracts later) – for example, you can agree to start out at an hourly rate and move to a retainer after a set amount of time or trial period of working together.

To summarize, it's definitely a good idea to start out with an hourly rate. But remember that you shouldn't necessarily stay there for the duration of your work with a client. Got it? Great!

Next, let's move on to figuring out what that hourly rate should be.

How Much Do You Need (Want) To Earn?

I mentioned the idea of "charging what you're worth" earlier. For a lot of people, this can be challenging to figure out in the beginning.

Money can be a difficult topic to discuss. But the bottom line is that we're doing business here, and it's going to come up in every discussion you have with a potential client. Remember that you're starting your business with a goal in mind. You, your time, and your services are valuable and worthy of being paid for – and paid well.

Having a firm grasp on what you're going to charge will help you enter into these client discussions more clearly and confidently. And like being clear on the services you offer, this will build your credibility and legitimacy as a professional.

So how do you figure out where to start with your rates?

Before we get into some numbers, there are some factors to take into consideration. Let's take a look.

1. Factor in Self-Employment

Keep in mind that as a self-employed individual (at least in the US), you'll need to pay both the employee and the employer side of taxes (self-employment tax). This may vary in other parts of the world, but there are typically these kinds of expenses to factor in no matter where you live.

Other self-employment expenses might include health care and other benefits, like saving for your retirement. You'll also need to be able to cover yourself financially for any sick days or time off that you need to take from your business.

For this reason, I recommend inflating the starting rate you come up with by 25% to cover these expenses. Remember that for a business, one of the major perks of hiring a VA is the low cost on their end, such as not having to pay for all the expenses associated with traditional employees. But this doesn't mean that you should be the cheapest solution out there.

2. Can You Include Gaining Experience in Your Pay?

What if you find a client who is willing to hire you and train you in new skills that you'll then be able to market to other potential clients? Should you include this in your rate of pay and be willing to charge slightly less?

Sure! If you can swing it, this is a great opportunity. But don't do this forever. You're starting this business to make money, and whether it's full-time or a side income, you still need to earn a wage that will work for you.

And I really don't recommend working for free. You may have an opportunity to do a practice project for a friend to gain some experience and market yourself with your results. This isn't necessarily a bad way to go in the very beginning. But don't enter into a long-term working relationship working for free or in exchange for training, unless you have tons of time on your hands and don't need the money.

3. How Much Can the Client Afford?

There's a balance point with rates. You don't want to charge so much that no one will hire you. But you definitely don't want to undercut yourself.

You're working within a client's budget, and they're hiring you so that they can save themselves time and money to be able to grow their business further. A client isn't going to be able to pay you the same rate they'd pay themselves. That just doesn't make sense for them from a return-on-investment (ROI) perspective, at least in most cases.

So while you don't want to charge too low a rate, you do want to take into account what is realistic and reasonable for the type of clients you're working with. In other words, if you're working for the local coffee shop owner, you're not going to be able to charge as much as you would if you were targeting high-level executives with your services.

Calculating Your Hourly Rate

A good way to determine your hourly rate is to consider what will make it worth your time and effort.

This is going to look different for everyone, depending on your current circumstances and where you want to end up. For example, someone looking to replace their full-time income will have a different lens for figuring out rates than someone looking to create some side income.

If you're looking to replace your current salary, figure out what your salary equates to on an hourly basis.

The most accurate way to do this is to take your annual salary and divide it by 26 (the number of pay periods in a year). Then, divide that number by 80 (the number of hours in a pay period).

For example, if you make $50,000 per year right now:

- $50,000 divided by 26 (pay periods) = $1,923 per pay period
- $1,923 divided by 80 (hours) = $24 per hour

And if you were to multiply that hourly wage by 125%, it would equal $30 per hour.

So if you're currently making $24 per hour, you'd need to charge at least $30 per hour in order to replace your salary from a self-employed standpoint. This includes inflating for that extra 25% we talked about earlier.

If you're not looking to replace a salary, give some thought to what would make this worth it to you. You can also take into consideration your "happiness number" – what hourly rate would make you feel happy about showing up every day?

You may also need to take into consideration any costs that come with running your business, like childcare, for example.

And lastly, you can think about your desired hourly rate from the perspective of the financial goals you have, like paying down debt, bringing in a certain amount of income to your household each month, or saving for something important to you. Given the time you have to dedicate to your business, how much would you need to charge to achieve your goals in an amount of time that feels good to you?

Whatever rate you come up with, be sure to factor in the three things we covered earlier:

- self-employment benefits
- training into your pay
- remaining affordable so that you can realistically get clients.

Action Step

1. Using the calculations and factors above, decide on the hourly rate you'd like to start with.

※ ※ ※

Like any of the steps we'll cover in this book, I encourage you to not get stuck on this one.

Figuring out the money part of starting a business and attaching a dollar amount to your time and skill can be either difficult or exciting. Remember that what you charge is ultimately up to you. And like any aspect of your business, nothing is set in stone.

Remember that you can, and should be, raising your rates with each new client you take on, as well as your existing clients after a period of time. Your initial rate is just a starting point. As you gain experience and hone your skills, you'll want to raise your rates accordingly.

We're looking to get you into profit mode as soon as possible, so settle on a rate to get started with. The sky is the limit. Starting a service-based business is the best way to break in online, and you never know where this adventure could take you!

In the next chapter, we're going to cover how to tell the world that you're in business.

Are you ready?

5

PREPARE YOUR ONLINE PRESENCE

So far, we've gone through some basic but important building blocks of your business:

- **Your mindset** – You've made a great decision. Quality VAs are in high demand, and there is unlimited potential when it comes to pursuing a specialty and commanding premium rates. You've also set some goals for your business, and you know where you want to go.
- **Your skills and chosen service** – You should be clear about what you're going to offer as a service and feel confident that you're coming into this with at least one existing skill (likely more) that will make you a great VA.
- **Your rates** – You should have a clear idea of where you'll be starting with your hourly rate as well as your future income potential.

Now it's time to talk about officially establishing yourself in the online world as a Virtual Assistant.

What Is an Online Presence?

As you're looking for your first clients, you'll want to have somewhere to send prospects so they can learn more about you and what you can do for them. Your "online presence" is simply where and how clients can find out about you. So it's worth taking the time to put something together.

There are various ways to go about finding clients, which we'll explore in the next chapter. While you can begin actively searching for clients before you've built your online presence, it's also a good idea to spend a little time setting up shop. That way, when you do come across those first prospects, you already have some credibility as a VA.

While an online presence may sound a little daunting to some, it doesn't need to be a massive undertaking. In fact, it shouldn't be if your goal is to land your first client as quickly as possible.

The bottom line is that in most industries these days, people are doing business, interacting, and communicating online. Having some kind of presence legitimizes you and makes you "real."

Three Ways To Establish Your Online Presence

We're going to cover a few ways you can go about establishing an online presence, from simple to a little more involved. Since our goal is to get you up and running quickly, I'm going to recommend starting with a simple plan and encourage you to build on that once you have those first few clients and can spend some time cultivating your business.

Ready? Let's explore the ways to build your online presence.

1. A Traditional Resume

When I say traditional resume, what comes to mind? A two-page document on fancy paper with organized bullet points and lots of jargon? That's not what we're going for here.

While in the 9-5 world resumes still hold some weight, in the online world they should look a little different. Why? Attention spans are very short, business owners are busy, and no one has the time or desire to read lots of words that don't actually say much.

In this case, a traditional resume would be a document highlighting your skills as they're relevant to the service you're offering and from the perspective of what you can do for business owners.

So what would this look like, and how would it be different?

To start off, I recommend drafting your resume as a Word document or Google Doc and then downloading it as a PDF. This can be attached to an email pitch or online application.

The first thing that someone should see is how to contact you. Make it super simple. You can even include a headshot to put a face to the name and make your resume stand out.

Next, while you can still include any education, it won't be as front-and-center as on a traditional resume. And if you don't have any, don't stress. These days, clients are more interested in what you can actually do for them than whether or not you've been to college.

If you do have some formal education, include it, but put it in a smaller section towards the bottom. The same goes for your work experience. Don't list out every single job you've ever had, but rather highlight your professional experience as it pertains to VA work.

This brings us to what should be the bulk of your resume – your experience as it relates to the service you're offering. For example, if you're offering customer service, I'd recommend having "Customer Service Experience" as a heading with relevant jobs, experiences, and any applicable training listed underneath.

And if you can, identify results-oriented experience, as in, "Managed a client base of 100 customers for X business."

Lastly, if you have any relevant certifications or training, list them. Include those that aren't directly related to your service but speak to who you are and what you can do. This could also become more relevant as you move forward in your journey and hone your skills.

Sandy, a past student of our course #FullyBookedVASystem,[1] started using a resume when she first began pitching clients. She made a clear bulleted list of her relevant skills followed by her experience. Even though Sandy has been in the traditional workforce for a long time, she only listed her VA experience followed by one job that she had worked for 15 years which provided her a ton of relevant skills.

In a smaller section on the left-hand side of Sandy's resume, she included her education. But she put her VA-related coursework at the top of the list and other certifications and education following.

The point? Sandy has lots of experience in the traditional work world but did a great job of pulling what a business owner would care about into a concise, relevant list.

In summary, here's what I'd recommend including on a resume:

- Contact information and headshot
- Relevant experience
- Certifications and/or trainings
- Education

Here are some things to keep in mind:

1. Your resume should be one to two pages (ideally one) focusing on skills versus education and work experience. You can still mention these, but they shouldn't be the primary focus.
2. Keep things relevant – not everything on your resume needs to be directly related to your VA business, and it is a good

idea to give prospects an idea of your personality. But do keep it relevant. Think about what would be interesting or valuable to know about you from a business owner's perspective.
3. It's okay to tailor your resume to a specific client you're pitching. Always be truthful, but don't over-exaggerate. Building a business on integrity, even in the tiniest of details, always wins out in the long run.
4. Make your resume stand out with a headshot. You can do this on your own or have a friend take one. It doesn't need to be professionally done, just professional looking. You can also use a pop of color and even add a logo if you're feeling fancy and know how to make one yourself. Just don't overdo it with the fancy stuff, which leads me to my next point...
5. Make sure it's easy and pleasant to read, not too cluttered, and definitely not overwhelming.

A resume isn't my number one tool for establishing a quick and easy online presence. But it can be helpful to get yourself thinking in the context of being a VA and organizing your information and skills. The result is that you'll be more confident about what you have to offer and about putting yourself out there to prospective clients.

Clients do ask for resumes from time to time, so it's not a bad idea to have one on hand. This is just one option, and it may not be for everyone, so don't get stuck here.

Now on to what is my recommended go-to for establishing a quick and easy online presence...

2. Maximize Your Social Media Profile

When it comes to getting yourself up and running on the internet as quickly as possible, using social media is a great way to go. I specifically recommend using LinkedIn and/or Facebook.

In the case of LinkedIn, you essentially have an online resume laid out for you. All you need to do is fill in the information. The other reason I like using these two platforms is that they're both an excellent place to find clients (more on this in the next chapter). So having an optimized profile on one or both is a no-brainer when it comes to sourcing clients.

Mera, another past student, recently had this win to share in our community:

So I just made my Facebook page, and sent a message to a few friends... and one immediately texted me and asked why she hadn't heard about this yet. She hired me (SQUEE!!) to handle her inbox and organize her cloud storage for her business. So, yea, um there's that. 28 days after I signed up...

All Mera had to do was set up a Facebook business page specific to her new VA business, message a few friends, and bam – she had her first client!

If you choose to go down this route, take the time to set up a profile specific to your VA business like Mera did. You can do this with a regular LinkedIn profile, or you can opt for a business profile – either is fine. On Facebook, you would set up a business page for your business. Don't forget to link your personal Facebook profile to your Facebook page.

A brief word about using social media for your business: if you choose this option, keep in mind that even if you create separate business pages or accounts for your VA business, potential clients will check you out personally as well.

Does this mean you need to turn your life over to your business? No. But do be aware that what you post on your personal page is a reflection of your overall character. In our digital age, people pay attention to these things, especially when it comes to trusting the integrity of someone they're thinking about hiring.

If you already have a LinkedIn profile and/or Facebook business page, spend some time optimizing them with the pointers below. If you don't have any, now is the perfect time to set one up!

1. For your profile picture, use a good headshot of your face only. In this case "good" means: well lit, taken by a friend if possible (versus a selfie), professional looking, (i.e., brush your hair, put on a nice top, etc.), and without a distracting background. Remember, you can do this with a phone camera.

2. Create a banner/header image with a non-distracting visual. Canva is a free tool that has templates for both LinkedIn and Facebook, so the size is just right for both platforms. Include your name and a tagline or the service(s) you're offering.

3. For LinkedIn, come up with a good headline that includes your primary service offering. Don't just say "Virtual Assistant." This is a great opportunity to stand out and grab some attention. You can also work this into your Facebook business "About" section.

Here's a good way to come up with an attention-grabbing headline:

I help _____ [WHO – business owners, or a certain type of business owner?] achieve/do _____ [RESULTS – what will your services do for them?] through/by/with _____ [YOUR SERVICE OFFERING].

If this is feeling challenging, just go with "[INSERT TOP SERVICE] Virtual Assistant" and circle back to this later.

4. Write a great About section. This will include:

- Your headline statement
- The types of clients you like to work with (if you don't know yet, leave this for now)
- What types of results you get or pain points you solve for clients
- Why working with you is different/your philosophy
- How they can reach out to work with you

5. For LinkedIn, fill out the rest of the sections. List positions and experience for at least the last five years. Then, select skills most rele-

vant to the work you want to do for now and showcase personal/professional awards in the "Accomplishments" section.

Here are some more pointers for setting up your profile(s) and establishing a presence on social media for your business:

- Make sure that someone can look at your profile and instantly see who you are, what you're offering, and how they can get a hold of you – an email address is fine for now.
- In your bio/about section, highlight your strengths and previous relevant experience (after your attention-grabbing headline). You can always (and should) go back in and add wins you're experiencing with clients.
- Make sure you've sized things appropriately for the platform. Fuzzy, distorted images won't make a good first impression.
- Get the basics of your profile(s) in place now. When you're ready, go back and add in a simple logo and some branding colors. Just make sure these are consistent across the platforms you use if there is more than one.
- Make sure your profiles are complete. This is essentially free advertising for your new VA business, so make the most of the space offered.

Once you've set up a profile, you can begin posting content that's relevant to your business. Focus on what is interesting, valuable, and engaging to the kinds of clients you want to attract. To get started, this could include blog posts (you've written or that are relevant to your audience, but noncompetitive to your service offerings), podcasts, helpful "how-to" pointers (time management, etc.), and content that speaks to your professional personality and philosophy in business.

I'd recommend posting once per day on weekdays. Consistency is key and helps establish that you're a legitimate professional.

It's also not a bad idea to spend some time looking around platform(s) and seeing what other VAs are doing that seems effective and engaging. The goal isn't to steal other's ideas but rather to be inspired about where you want to take your own social media presence in the context of your business.

Alum Leslie of "Clarity Virtual Support" posts a variety of content on her Facebook business page. For example, her posts include:

- Announcements about industry-relevant developments, like a WordPress plugin created by Google, for example
- Helpful resources, such as screen-time management tools for parents
- Inspiring quotes
- Interesting information about work she's doing with clients
- Engaging personal stories
- Occasional posts that highlight the type of services she's providing and promote her business.

We'll talk more about how to use social media to build your business in the next chapter. But for now, remember that this is your opportunity to paint yourself in the most positive light and highlight your awesomeness.

3. Create a Website With a Hire Me Page

I'm going to say the least about this option. Why? Because our goal is to land that first client within a few weeks, and I've seen many a new VA get stuck here. But a website isn't a bad idea, so I do want to give you some forward-focused info about building your online presence with a website.

Let me say this first: you don't need a website to get started.

In fact, three out of the four most recent success stories we've featured on the Horkey HandBook blog were VAs who didn't even have websites when they started offering services. And yet, they've built successful, thriving businesses.

For our purposes, I'd discourage creating a website for now. But I do encourage you to consider one in the future once you have a few clients and are looking to build your business further. A website is a great opportunity to have somewhere to send clients and really highlight you, your business, and what you can do for them. It's also an excellent way to practice a newfound skill set around website setup and maintenance.

Having said that, if you already have a website or blog, you can always rebrand it to suit your VA business. I highly recommend doing this so it's not confusing to prospective clients. In that case, you'll want to add a Hire Me page to make it clear to prospects what it is you do and that you're currently for hire.

If you don't have a website yet, don't worry about it. Just know that in the future if you decide to create one, a good Hire Me page is crucial. Here's what to include:

1. An introduction, including that headline we talked about in the previous social media section
2. A bio and headshot
3. A "hire me" video where you talk about what you can do for a business
4. Your service(s)
5. Your rates
6. A call to action – "Click this button to connect," for example
7. A clear way to contact you
8. Client testimonials when you have them

In summary, if you're just getting started, store this info and come back to it after you've landed that first client or three.

Action Step

1. Choose one of the three ways to build your online presence.

* * *

Putting yourself out there and announcing to the online world that you're a VA is another exciting step in the process. It's yet another opportunity for things to become real. It can also help you further conceptualize your business and how you'd like to come across in the marketplace.

Creating a resume is an easy way to get started and provides something to put in the hands of prospective clients. A simple but professional PDF is a great way to go.

Establishing your business on social media is an excellent setup for branding your business, networking, and finding clients. Remember that it's not a "set it and forget it" scenario, though. Your profile should evolve as you do. And to really have an effective presence on social media, you need to actually spend some time cultivating it. If you're thinking about offering social media services, your own social media presence is also a must-have.

Lastly, a website is a great way to establish your business's legitimacy… when you're ready. It's absolutely not critical to starting a successful business. Many VAs build their client base and get to this later. If and when you decide you're ready for a website, remember that a good Hire Me page is crucial. It's got the most relevant information that prospective clients will want to know about you. It also helps them to easily take the next step when it comes to working with you.

You can choose one, two, or all three of these options. To land that first client in 30 days, I'd recommend going as simple as possible and choosing one for now. I always lean toward an optimized LinkedIn profile to start out. The bottom line is that it's a great opportunity to get creative, show your stuff, and stand out from the crowd.

In the next chapter, we're going to take the plunge. It's time to find your first client.

6

SOURCING PROSPECTS TO PITCH

So far, we've laid the foundation of your new VA business. If you've been following the action steps, you should have the basics in place to put yourself out there and find that first client.

Things like:

1. The service you'll offer
2. The rate you'll charge
3. Your online VA presence, i.e., your virtual "storefront"

It's time to open up those doors and officially put out your shingle as a Virtual Assistant! In this chapter we're going to cover three of the quickest, easiest ways to find that first client or two (and beyond). Keep in mind that there are a lot of ways to find clients.

Since I want you to find that first client as soon as possible, I've chosen the three methods I've seen new VAs succeed with time and time again. They also feel the most comfortable when you're just starting out.

Later in your business when you've really niched down your services and target market, you'll want to explore some more focused ways of sourcing high-quality clients. This is a valuable aspect of investing in yourself – pursuing further training and information so that you can really scale your business to the maximum.

For now, let's focus on simple and straightforward. Before we get into those three methods I mentioned, let's spend a minute addressing something really important: your mindset around sourcing clients.

Your Client-Finding Mindset

First of all, how do you feel about actually putting yourself out there and finding clients? Is it, *Let's do this thing!* or is it, *Gulp. Okay, I guess I'm ready...?*

If it's the former, that's great – let's go! And if it's the latter, you'll be fine, promise. And if it's a combination of the two, that's fine too.

This is another exciting, concrete step toward making your goals a reality. I want you to get out there and find that first client right away. It's helpful to head into this part of your journey with a few key things in mind.

1. If You're Not Looking for Clients...

You're not going to find them!

Here's the thing: sourcing clients to pitch is the lifeblood of your business! Clients aren't going to come knocking on your virtual door. When you're just starting out and don't have client work to fill your time with yet, your primary task should be finding potential clients to pitch. We'll cover exactly how to pitch in the next chapter.

For now, take the time you've carved out in your schedule for client work and spend it finding clients. Once you've landed a client or two, prioritize your time by taking care of your client work first. Then, keep focusing on finding more clients with whatever time you have left over.

To give you a sneak peek down the not-too-distant future of your business, you'll want to source and pitch clients until your roster is full. And then? It's still not a bad idea to continue sourcing clients!

I've found that new VAs can get really excited about the "business building" stuff, such as putting their business basics in place. And for good reason – it's new and fun! I've also found that when it comes to actually finding that first client, some new VAs procrastinate by focusing on every tiny detail of the basics before they feel ready to put themselves out there.

Don't let this be you. You can put in place what we've covered so far within a day and start looking for that first client immediately. You can always circle back and take care of details later. Remember, we want to get you into profit, pronto!

2. Always Be Marketing

What do I mean by this? Specifically that you're in it to win it with this VA thing. So start keeping your eyes open for opportunities. Then, never shut them. If you adopt the lens of someone with a valuable service who legitimately helps business owners, you'll start to see potential in places you never thought of.

Imagine you're at your local mechanic, and you notice they have a Facebook page. You could take a peek while you're waiting for your oil to be changed and find that their presence is somewhat dismal. This is often the case with many small business owners who know they need to be on social media but don't want to deal with it. So you mention that you could help them with that if social media is your thing. Easy peasy, right?

Keep your eyes open, and more importantly, listen for opportunities. Don't be afraid to strike up conversations, whether it's in person at a business you frequent or networking on social media. Authentically listen for those opportunities where you can be of assistance.

For example, maybe you notice a business owner on social media complaining of being stressed. You can comment and then drop them a direct message offering to help! The worst that could happen would be you get a "no." But if you don't ask, the answer is always no. At best you may end up with a new client who appreciates that you were paying attention and showed up at just the right time.

Want to know how I found my first client? I purchased an online course from a well-known webpreneur, and we had an email exchange. While emailing back and forth, I noticed that he had difficulty getting back to me but really seemed to want to!

Specifically, he was apologetic about his response time, and it was clear to me that email management wasn't his passion. So I asked him to hire me! Here's how it went:

B,

I think you really need to hire me! I'm uber-organized and could keep you on task, cover for you when things like a sick child come up, and help you to take your business to the next level.

Are you looking to expand your team with a Virtual Assistant? You probably like to handle your own email (hence you always responding to me), but maybe that's not the best idea. You're a hustler and in the midst of building something big – let me help you!

Figure I have nothing to lose in asking,

~Gina

And you know what? He said yes. I suggested some ways to get started, asked a few questions, and proposed a two-week trial period and rate over the phone. He agreed, and we set up a video call to meet and get things set up.

We worked happily together for about three years.

3. Believe in Yourself

You've made the decision to do this, so own it. Embrace the fact that you can help businesses and that there are plenty out there that need your help. You just need to be on the lookout.

When you're excited and confident about what you're doing, it will come through in the way that you talk with people. If you believe, they'll believe – and want to hire you! Confidence and enthusiasm go a long way when it comes to assuring a potential client that you're the solution they're looking for.

Take Ashley from our private community, for example. She landed her first client after sharing her excitement about her new business with someone at her local dog park. Potential clients are everywhere!

Remember to be your authentic self. You don't need to "sell yourself" to just anyone. In fact, you don't want to work with just anyone, not even as a first client, or take on work that you know you'll hate, at a terrible rate, just to get started. Just keep in mind that you don't need to be "salesy." You have something awesome to offer to the right client, so let your confidence shine through.

Now that you have your mindset ready, you're raring to get out and find your first client, right? Let's explore three ways to do that.

Method 1: Ask People You Know if They Need Help

Ever heard that saying, "Your network is your net worth"? When it comes to finding potential clients, this couldn't be truer.

Starting conversations with people in your immediate network is one of the most common ways I've seen new VAs land their first client. This may initially feel uncomfortable for some, as it brings up visions of listing 100 of your friends to sell Tupperware to. But with the right approach, it doesn't have to be awkward or off-putting at all.

I understand the apprehension that can come with talking to people in your immediate network about what it is you're doing. In my former life as a financial advisor, I was trained to start this way, and it was very uncomfortable.

I was taught to invite people from my network to come in for a free consultation, offer value specific to their situation, and go in for the kill. Then, I also asked them for referrals. It was pretty direct, and as I said, uncomfortable. But it also worked.

I built my financial advising business this way, and it accomplished a couple of things:

- It forced me outside my comfort zone – this is always where the good stuff happens.
- It let people know what I was doing and legitimized my business – there was no way I was going to put myself out there like that and fail in six months.

That said, I'm going to encourage you to take a different approach. Specifically, instead of asking people for their business, ask them for their help.

Take inventory of some people in your current circle that would be relevant to what you're doing, i.e., either they own a business or might know people who do. Ideally, these would be people close to you that you could connect with via email, or even better, in person.

Ask them if they're available to chat via phone or in person and share your big news with them. Tell them why you're getting into VA work and what you hope to accomplish. Then, ask for their advice.

People (especially those connected to you) generally love to help and give advice. Be authentic in your desire to hear from them – you never know what wisdom you'll walk away with. Don't be afraid to ask them about their ideas for marketing your business. If they don't have any, no problem. You're doing your homework and just thought you'd ask.

Your goal is to let them know about your intentions in building your new business. As you're wrapping things up, politely ask if they'll keep you in mind should they know of any small business owners that might be looking for help.

And the more specific you are, the better!

For example: *Can you keep me in mind if you know of a self-employed friend who is looking for help, but isn't ready to hire a part- or full-time employee? Often they are the best fit for a VA like myself. And I especially love to do XYZ tasks.*

Be sure to make the conversation even more about them as it is about you. Ask about their family, business, whatever is most meaningful in their life currently, and listen. Ask if there's any way you can help or be of service to them.

And lastly, don't forget to follow up and thank them for their time and input. They might not have had a need, or they may have had someone else top of mind when you talk. But an authentic chat that showed that you valued their input followed with a personalized "thank you" will keep you top of mind when an opportunity comes up.

My friend and Horkey HandBook teammate, Laura, landed her first client by reaching out to her immediate network. She wrote a blog post about horses and used it as a great reason to reach out to a friend she hadn't talked to in years who owned a ranch and horseback riding business. It also helped that she had quoted him in the post and wanted to share it with him.

As it turned out, he was happy to hear about Laura's new business venture and offer some words of advice and encouragement. He also needed some help with his Facebook presence.

Since Laura knew enough to be able to make a difference for him and was a really quick learner, they've had a successful working relationship for over three years now. He's also referred her to other business owners which resulted in two more clients for her VA business.

Method 2: Put Yourself Out There on Social Media

Remember in the last chapter when we discussed using social media as a way to build your online presence? Well, with an optimized profile, you can also be more proactive with social media and use it to source clients.

In fact, this method is also how I've seen many new VAs find their first clients. I've even heard of being hired through direct message correspondences after commenting on a post and reaching out to the business owner behind it – more than once, I might add.

Natalie, a past student, started her search for clients by networking in Facebook groups. She responded to a comment she saw on a post in one of the groups, reached out directly, and landed her first client all through direct messaging!

And Cindy from our VA Leads Community had this fun story to share about landing her first client on social media: ... *she found me from a post I put in a Facebook group for entrepreneurs stating that I was trying to get over my fear of finding that first client. Who knew?*

Social media can also be another source of your network I just talked about in the last section. In our digital age, it's common to make connections and form friendships via social media with people we've never even met in person. If you have these connections already, reach out to them!

There are three ways I'd go about putting yourself out there on social media.

1. Posting

After you've set up your profile on Facebook or LinkedIn (these are the two I'd focus on for now), start posting consistently with some of the ideas we covered in the last chapter.

The goal of consistent posting is letting folks know who you are and what you do, and that you're a real person who shows up regularly. You're not a flake.

We're going to take it one step further, though, with a direct post about your services. You can post something like the example below a few times a month (change up your wording though) without feeling obnoxious about it, especially if you've been posting other content regularly.

I'd also recommend posting this on your personal profile. You likely have more connections built up over there at this point compared to your new Facebook page. Let your friends and connections know what you're doing – you never know what may come of it.

Here's an example of a post:

Know anyone that needs help with [insert your service]?

I help people with these tasks as a Virtual Assistant from my home office.

Currently, I have room to take on one more client.

If you (or someone you know) could use some help in this department, feel free to direct message me or share this post.

I appreciate YOU!

2. Groups

Facebook and LinkedIn groups can be a gold mine for finding clients. Spend some time finding and joining groups for business owners and entrepreneurs that look like places you could "hang out." Set aside a certain amount of time per day for networking in these groups.

Specifically, read through posts and comment with encouragement and helpful input when appropriate – like Natalie did! Become a presence in these groups so that when someone posts that they're looking for help, you can respond as an authentic professional rather than a lurker who is client-hunting.

3. Networking

Networking really goes hand in hand with interacting in groups. But the concept, in general, is applicable to everything you do with social media. It's not enough to throw some posts out there. You need to spend time cultivating relationships and having conversations.

Build relationships by interacting on comments and reaching out through direct conversations. Don't get lost in Social Media Land, but do carve out time for this activity. It's definitely worth the effort, and you never know who you'll come across that could change your whole world.

Method 3: Search the Internet

There is an unlimited number of businesses to pitch your services to on the internet. This method involves knowing what kinds of businesses need the services you're offering so you can narrow your search. We'll cover how to pitch them in the next chapter.

There are two ways to go about this:

1. Find interesting-looking businesses and immediately pitch them
2. Take some time to make a connection and "woo" them before pitching

I'd recommend some combination of the two, depending on your impression of the businesses you find.

To get started, spend some time researching businesses that look intriguing and realistic to you. LinkedIn is a great place to start with this. You might come across companies who are clearly seeking or are open to help, while it might not be so obvious with others.

In the former case – pitch them right away!

In the latter case, you'd want to spend a little time making a connection first. One way to do that would be by reaching out via email with a simple hello and kind (authentic) comment about a blog post or email you received, for example. If you saw an opportunity, you could also offer some helpful, relevant information. And you could also connect via social media and begin the conversation that way.

Showing a business that you're authentically interested in what they're doing puts you on their radar. The point here is to lead with value and make an impression before pitching them anything you have to offer.

Action Step

1. Make a list of 10 potential clients to reach out to.

* * *

While laying the foundation of your business is exciting and valuable, sourcing clients to pitch is the first step you'll take to directly turn your actions into income. Embrace what you're doing and own it. When you put out that confidence and energy into your interactions, you tend to attract what it is you're looking for. And in this case, it's that first client to kick off your new VA business!

You have at your fingertips three actionable, easy ways to find your first client. If you're feeling a little bit nervous at this point, you're not alone. Remember that while this may be slightly out of your comfort zone, that's exactly where you want to be and right where the good stuff happens.

Now that you have your list of potential clients, let's walk through how to pitch them.

7

SEND YOUR FIRST FEW PITCHES

After spending some time researching and finding prospective clients, it's time to actually reach out and pitch your awesome service! This is where putting yourself out there takes on a whole new meaning.

By preparing your online presence as we covered in Step Four, you started the process of establishing yourself as a legitimate VA – someone with a valuable, needed service to offer businesses. This step is setting up your virtual storefront.

But as we covered in the last chapter, your customers aren't going to come looking for you. You need to go out and find them! And not only do you need to find them, but you also need to let them know why they should consider bringing you into their business.

In this chapter we'll cover what a pitch is, what important elements should be included, and pitching best practices. With great pitching skills, you'll stand out and get noticed as the professional you are.

What Is a Pitch?

A pitch is simply a way of asking to be hired. In the first four steps, you began working *on* your business. But like sourcing clients, pitching them is one of the first steps you'll take *in* your business. Like sourcing clients, pitching truly is the lifeblood of your business.

After finding potential clients to reach out to, pitching is your opportunity to connect with them in a professional and memorable way. It's where you get to bring together the time and energy you've put into formulating your business and actually land some paying work.

If you're feeling intimidated by the idea of offering your service to potential clients, go back and read the last chapter. While it's normal to experience some nerves about asking to be hired, it gets easier and easier with time as your confidence grows, especially after you land that first paying client.

Remember that we're doing business here. There is nothing inappropriate, odd, or annoying about offering your service to a company that you perceive may benefit from it.

While you may experience a few "nos" before you get a "yes" – or even several – know that every pitch matters. Each one is an opportunity to gain more confidence and learn how to do things a little better.

Taryn, another past student, had a great mindset when pitching her first client:

I made my first cold pitch to a graphic designer that I've been following on Instagram for some years now. And Gina was right – it was fun. There was no risk, and the only bad thing that could've happened would be that she says no. I think it was easier for me than I thought because I believe in the product I'm selling!

Once you get over the initial self-limiting thoughts you might be having, pitching can actually be fun! And sometimes amazing things happen, as they did for Christine:

I just landed my first long-term client!!! I sent her a cold pitch yesterday, and she emailed me back less than an hour later saying I was hired – we talked pricing and what services she needed, and she just sent an email to her team introducing me!

Pretty awesome, right?!

Now that we've covered what a pitch is, let's look at what you should include in yours.

Elements of a Pitch

Your pitches are most likely going to be sent via email. Depending on how you're sourcing clients, you may end up submitting a form or application through a site if you choose to explore marketplaces like Upwork. But for our purposes, we're going to focus on pitching via email. Are you ready?

1. Subject Line

Keep in mind that when you send an email to a business owner, they're most likely very busy and probably get many emails each day. So for that reason, you'll want your first point of contact to stand out in a potential sea of emails.

An effective subject line can be a matter of trial and error, but I recommend going with simple and catchy. You want to spark some interest and get your email opened but not sound spammy.

Whenever possible, try and get the first name of the person you're emailing, ideally the owner of the business, and include it in your subject line. It's a great way to stand out from all the other emails that are probably coming through in the course of a day.

Here are some examples:

1. This one is casual and sounds like you're sending an email to a friend:

Hey/Heyya/Howdy [name], quick question for you...

2. This one is obvious about your intent, but still casual and fun:

Kickass (or other adjective of your choice) VA obsessed with [company name]

3. This one shows confidence and is still fun and to the point:

[Company name] and a [adjective] VA, let's make magic together!

4. This one is simple, not too "in your face," but still solid:

[Name], got five minutes?

And a couple more…

[Company or person's name], you and I would make a great team!

[Name], I love [insert something cool about the company, recent blog post you liked, etc.]!

2. The Body of Your Pitch

First of all, keep in mind that your pitch is your first professional point of contact with a business owner, and first impressions are everything. Check your spelling and grammar (you can use a free tool like Grammarly) and communicate in a personable but professional tone. Leave out emojis and overly casual language, but try to come across as friendly and someone who would be pleasant to work with.

Next, be clear and concise – don't write a novel; no one has the time or desire to read it. Open up with something personalized to the business you're pitching that indicates you've actually spent time learning about the company. And don't forget that a little authentic flattery will get you everywhere.

Perhaps use something along the lines of, "I've spent some time on your website and really appreciate the culture of your company and how you communicate that in your mission statement."

Follow by getting down to brass tacks – who you are and what you do. Rather than go on and on about yourself (again, no one wants to read that), speak to the business owner about what you can do for them when you're talking about your service.

Then, let them know where they can go to find out more about you. That way you're leaving it up to them rather than cramming your life story into an email. Attach your resume and link to your VA-focused social media profile(s) or even your Hire Me page on your website if you have one.

3. Include a Call To Action

You want to make things simple and straightforward for the business owner you're pitching. Remember that they're busy. This is your opportunity to show them right off the bat how smooth you can make things for them versus confusing and annoying.

Tell them exactly what the next step is – to continue the conversation and/or schedule a few minutes to chat and see if you'd be a good fit for each other. Notice I didn't say anything about working for them.

Present yourself as someone who brings something to the table they need to make their life easier. Exude confidence, which will encourage their faith that you can do this. And you can.

You're not begging for work here. You're offering them an opportunity that could make their life easier and their company run more efficiently.

In your call to action, give them a *very* clear way to get in touch with you and to schedule time to chat. I recommend setting up a free account with Calendly and putting the link to your calendar in your email so they can just go right in and schedule time. It cuts down on the back-and-forth of "what time/days work for you?"

You can also say something like "hit reply to continue the conversation" and communicate via email, which some business owners may prefer over hopping on a call right away. They may have questions to ask and would prefer an email exchange to get the ball rolling.

The point is to make it super clear and easy for them to get in touch with you!

Some Pitching Examples

In the last chapter, we talked about reaching out to your network. While I encouraged you to connect face-to-face whenever possible, we're also focused on finding that first client as quickly as possible. So email may be a more efficient way to go about connecting for now.

Here's an example of an email reaching out to an existing contact/friend:

Hey Friend,

I don't know if you're aware, but I've been busy building an online business recently. One of the ways that I want to help people is as a Virtual Assistant.

You might already know, but a few of my more prominent skills are in the area of [insert your service offering].

The funny thing is that a lot of small business owners struggle with this. I've found that [insert your target market or stick with "small business owners" for now] are a great fit especially, based on my previous experience as [insert why].

I was wondering if you'd keep me in mind if you ever come across a [insert target market or a similar small business owner] that is looking for help, but not ready to hire a part-time or full-time employee? A Virtual Assistant is an excellent fit for someone like that.

They don't have to provide benefits, vacation, or sick time, or pay employment taxes when working with me. And we can start with just a few hours a week and build from there as it makes sense. Lastly, since I work virtually, they don't have to find a spot for me in their office.

I'm really excited about using my current skills to help others grow their businesses. If you know someone, feel free to pass on my phone number or introduce us via email. I'd really appreciate it!

~[Your Name]

And if you've researched some businesses to reach out to, here's an example of an email you could send as a pitch:

Hi [Business owner name],

I've been thinking about reaching out to you for some time. I've been learning about your business and really appreciate [Insert something personalized about their business, i.e., something you learned from their website, blog, or social media profile].

Honestly, I've been a little timid to connect before now, because I didn't know how you'd react to me offering my help. Sometimes I think that successful people like yourself don't sleep or something, and that's how they "do it all."

But then I thought that maybe you're struggling at times to keep up? And maybe I could help?

I could help in growing [insert business name] by providing [insert service].

This would help you:

- *1. [What your service would do for them – keep their inbox clear and manageable? Build a presence on social media and drive traffic to their website?]*
- *2. [Save time, for example]*
- *3. [Free you up to work on high-level tasks in your business to impact your bottom line, for example]*

What do you think?

Are you ready to delegate some tasks that you don't like to do (or don't have time for), increase the ROI of your business, and enjoy your work more?

If so, just hit reply, and let's continue the conversation.

The next step would be to schedule some time to chat and see if we're a good fit for working with one another. If you're ready to go ahead and do that, you can schedule something here [hyperlink to your Calendly calendar].

You can find out more about me by [Insert way they can learn about you – resume, links to social media profile(s), and/or Hire Me page].

~[Your Name]

Keep in mind that these templates are to give you an idea of what a pitch should look like and that you should customize them to fit your own voice and style.

Pitching Best Practices

As you approach this very crucial part of your business, here are some things to keep in mind to help you head into pitching with the right mindset and to be as efficient and effective with your efforts as possible.

1. Start Now

Don't even wait until you finish this book! If you've been following along with the action steps so far, you officially have everything you need right now to find your first client.

2. Be Confident

You may feel like you're not qualified and may even be going through an "imposter syndrome" kind of feeling. That's normal. The truth is: to succeed you need to believe that you can learn quickly and figure things out.

To be clear, this is not about being arrogant or dishonest. It's about being assertive and owning what you're doing with an attitude of, "Of course I can handle XYZ for you," even if you need to look it up on Google or YouTube to figure it out.

3. Timing Is Everything

If you come across something that looks like a potential opportunity, such as a comment in a social media group, for example, jump on it. Don't wait and mull it over.

You never know who else is seeing the same opportunity. And the business that you reach out to will likely take notice that you're a mover and shaker and are on top of things. That's someone you want on your team.

4. Pitch at Least Once per Day

As I covered in the last chapter, finding clients and pitching them should be your number one priority for now. Make pitching a daily practice. Not only will you get better at it and gain confidence, but your efforts will have a cumulative effect. Put yourself out there consistently, and something is bound to happen.

5. Do Your Research

Sending out "blanket" emails that aren't personalized are not going to get you anywhere. While there is a ton of opportunities as a VA, we still operate in a competitive world. And you need to stand out.

Showing a business you've taken the time to learn something about them is the perfect way to start off on the right foot and establish that you're not a spammy marketer. And it doesn't have to take more than a few minutes.

6. Make Things Easy

Remember to make things as easy as possible for your potential client to get in touch with you and learn more about you. You want the path to your virtual doorstep to be smooth and seamless. This is another way to communicate right off the bat that you're a legit professional.

If you can run the show in your own business, including how you present yourself, you can definitely be of help and service to them.

7. Make Your Pitch About Them

Again, people want to hear about what you can do for them, not your entire work history or personal story. There's a creative way to present who you are and what you're offering from the lens of how it will impact their business.

8. Follow Up

Of all the best practices I'm sharing here, this may be the most important one.

If you're not following up with your pitches, you might as well not be sending them. I can't tell you how many VAs I've heard from that landed a gig because they followed up.

Remember Natalie from the last chapter? She started pitching about two weeks after taking the leap and built up her client roster quickly. Now she's running a VA agency with her sisters!

What's one of her secret weapons? Following up:

I let him know in my pitch that I'm a quick learner and told him about my other skills. I didn't hear back from him, so I sent a follow-up email, and guess what? He told me I was the only one to follow up with him!...

Consistency is the key! I've been sending several pitches a week – all video pitches – and then following up three days later. I cannot tell you how many times I've been thanked for following up!

Again, business owners are busy! They may have missed your first email or have forgotten to reply. Following up once a week for a few weeks, then once every couple of weeks, then monthly is a way of establishing that you're a professional and serious about doing business. Keep going until you hear a "no thanks" or a "yes!"

9. Don't Give Up!

This best practice tip is right up there in terms of importance. Remember that you are sowing seeds, and your consistency and diligence will pay off.

The only ones who fail at this are the ones who quit. Keep moving forward. If your pitches aren't getting a response for some reason, consider having a trusted friend take a look at one and give you some feedback. You may need to change your approach or your wording, but keep persisting. You will land that first client, and it'll just get easier from there.

Robin, another student, had this encouragement to share about landing her first client:

I pitched three clients; the first two I never heard back from, but the third I landed 36 hours after initial contact...

... for anyone curious, I found this client on a Canadian-specific VA group on Facebook. I joined a bunch of networking groups worldwide to expand the search pool, but I never thought I would land someone in my proverbial backyard (we live in the same province). You just never know where you will find a client, so stay open to all possibilities!

I should also mention I'm a total newbie at this and landed my first client without a website or video pitch, or anything fancy. I did make a lovely brochure, but that was the extent of it. The rest was based on old-fashioned job searching and interviewing skills and using my previous in-house work experience to draw on... I wasn't "ready" in the sense of having all the pieces together, but I forced myself out there anyway, and it still worked out.

So, to all the newbies: yes, it's scary to take that first step, but remind yourself of all the things you HAVE accomplished up to this point and be confident you CAN do this!

Action Step

1. Send two pitches each day, Monday through Friday.

* * *

You now officially have everything you need to look for that first client – or three! Yes, we have more to cover regarding what to do once you land your client. But for now, take a deep breath and just get started. You have nothing to lose and everything to gain!

Take some time to craft a pitching template that you can adapt for each pitch you send. You may also have more than one kind of pitch. Save it somewhere to make things easy for yourself. Keep these best practices in mind, pay attention to what seems to be working, and cultivate that. Sow those seeds, and you'll be reaping a harvest of success and achieving your goals!

Next, we'll explore what to do once you've successfully landed your first client.

8

LAND YOUR FIRST CLIENT

You've put some foundational pieces of your business in place, searched for potential clients to reach out to, and have pitched your service to them.

Congratulations! You've made your first official point of contact with potential clients. Now it's time to take things to the next level.

After all the excitement of getting things ready in your business and possibly overcoming some nerves with pitching, it's not uncommon to experience thoughts of *What do I do now?!* when you start hearing back from pitches. Don't worry, I've got you covered.

In this chapter I'll walk you through the next step in landing that first client. And like other steps in this book, it will get easier and easier each time you do it. With some consistency and practice, before you know it, you'll be onboarding like a pro and enjoying a full client roster!

What It Looks Like To Interview

If you're coming from the traditional 9-5 or corporate world, the thought of an interview may bring up mixed feelings for you.

First of all, erase any thoughts of walking into a stuffy room, sitting in front of a desk in a short chair, and describing a time you dealt with a difficult customer. When it comes to VA work, interviews are typically less formal. These exchanges are a more relaxed and casual – yet professional – exchange between two business owners.

Does that mean you shouldn't take them seriously? Definitely not. You did all of the work to get your foot in the door and the conversation started. This busy business owner is interested enough to take time out of their schedule to chat with you and hear what you have to say. So make the most of the opportunity.

Almost all interviews take place via phone, video call, or through email exchange. It's very rare that an interview would take place in person unless you had pitched your services to a local business owner who was interested in sitting down with you – which isn't a bad thing.

And it's not uncommon to seal the deal with a client completely through an email exchange. It happens all the time. If things do progress to chatting via phone call or video chat, keep in mind that your potential client most likely wants to get down to brass tacks, so it won't be a long, drawn-out experience. It's also a good idea to prepare ahead so you're making the most of the time for both of you.

Your Interviewing Mindset

As you head into your interview, it's important to keep in mind that this process goes both ways. You're interviewing your potential client as much as they're interviewing you.

By the time you get to the point of interviewing, it's likely that you've already hashed some things out via email. This process is really an opportunity for you both to explore whether you'd be a good fit for working with one another.

As I've mentioned in a previous chapter, many VAs have taken on clients they were less than thrilled about in the beginning of their businesses in order to gain experience and create income.

But also keep in mind that one of the perks of this business is showing up every day to do tasks you enjoy with people you love working alongside. Respecting and appreciating your clients makes all the difference in the world in terms of your motivation to do a great job.

So the point is, you don't want just any ol' client! Be sure that the working relationship you're about to enter into is a good fit for you and how you want to spend your time in your business.

Lastly, an interview is an opportunity to put a face to the name. It's a chance to meet either "face-to-face" or "voice-to-voice" and establish a personal connection. Remember that bringing someone into the inner workings of their business involves a significant trust factor for almost all business owners. Making a connection through an interview is a way to establish that "know, trust, and like" factor that will help a business owner decide whether they want to offer you the opportunity.

Interviewing Tips

I could give you dozens of interview tips, but let's focus on the most pertinent ones.

1. Be Professional

While we covered that VA interviews are typically more relaxed than traditional ones, it's important to make an effort to present professionally. This includes how you're communicating verbally as well as your appearance if you're interviewing via video chat.

Don't break out the business-casual pantsuit, but do put some effort into a neat and clean appearance. Whether you're interviewing via phone or video chat, do your best to be in a quiet, non-distracting space where you can focus on the conversation.

Keep in mind that a potential client is often considering you from the lens of how you'll represent their business to the public. Be personable and friendly and let your personality shine through. But be more professional than you would be with your friend next door.

2. Prepare Ahead of Time

There's nothing worse than getting to the point of an interview and then fumbling around verbally because you're nervous and/or unprepared. Write the owner's name (or whoever is interviewing you) and business name down and keep it in front of you just in case you draw a nervous blank.

It's also not a bad idea to do more digging into their company so you'll have it fresh in your mind when you chat. It will go a long way with your potential client if you show in an authentic, non-awkward way that you've taken the time to learn more about them. This is also great material for a relaxed, pleasant conversation. Remember that almost everyone likes to talk about themselves (in this case, their business), so it's an easy conversation piece.

3. Listen More Than You Talk

Some of us tend to get chatty when we get nervous. Don't let this be you. Your goal in an interview is to ask intelligent questions to get to know the business owner, what their business does, whom they serve, and how you can help them be more effective.

It's helpful to prepare some questions ahead of time (write them down) and listen. You'll have your opportunity to speak, and of course, your potential client will want to hear from you. But they'll also appreciate your sincere interest in them and their business and how you can support them.

Remember my friend and teammate Laura? When she started building her client roster, she found that her video pitches were getting a great response, but she wasn't getting too far when it came to the interviews.

When I asked her what kinds of questions she was asking during interviews, guess what? She realized that she wasn't really asking any. What's more, Laura could see that because she was nervous, she was doing most of the talking!

Once she made the shift to preparing questions ahead of time and listening more than she was talking, Laura's client roster literally filled up within a matter of weeks.

4. Stay Calm and Interview On

Lastly, chill out. Come in confident with a relaxed attitude and open mind. If this interview doesn't work out for some reason, chalk it up to great practice. Be assured that the right client is out there, and with your consistent focus and efforts, they will show up.

Find a way to relax beforehand by taking a walk, listening to your favorite tune, doing a few jumping jacks, or whatever your relaxation trick is. I highly recommend visualizing a confident, calm you breezing your way through the discussion with poise and professionalism.

And most of all, remember that you've got this!

Onboarding a New Client

So you rocked the interview and are ready to begin a working relationship with a new client. Great! You may have completed some kind of paid test project for them or agreed to start with a short trial period. Or maybe it's a yes right off the bat, and you're both ready to dig in and work together.

Now it's time to get down to business! My goal is to help you with a simple, streamlined onboarding process that will make things easier for you and provide your client with a great experience right away.

As a side note, there are all kinds of clients and personalities out there. Some clients may have worked with a VA before and will be crystal clear on how they want things to go. These clients are typically direct in the process. Your role here would be to take in what they're asking you to do and know when to raise your hand with a clarifying question.

On the other end of the spectrum, some clients know they need help, but have no idea what the process of working with a VA looks like. They'll be looking to you to get things going. While in some ways it's nice to start off with those more direct-style clients for learning purposes, you may find that you're starting with the latter type of client. So you'll need to show up with your onboarding process confidently in hand.

Here's my simple three-step onboarding process:

1. Get It in Writing

While you've agreed to work together, you may or may not have clarified some of the finer details of your role with your new client. You'll also want to gain your client's commitment to working together to really seal the deal.

I'll go into contracts later in this chapter, but for now, know that having an agreement in writing with the details of your working relationship is a great way to legitimize your new arrangement. It protects both you and your client. And it's a smart way to start things off on the right foot.

2. Gather Some Details

You've probably already learned quite a bit about your client so far, but as you're getting started, take some time to gather information that will help you carry out your tasks and contribute to a great working relationship.

This information could include:

- Their contact details, such as a mailing address and phone number
- Their preferred way of communicating, whether it's email or a team management platform like Slack or Asana

- Their social media handles and website URL
- What tools and programs they use and how to access them. If they prefer you to use their accounts versus setting one up for you, it's a good idea to use a tool like 1Password or LastPass for safe and secure password sharing.
- Whether they would like to have regular check-ins, how often, and on what platform (Zoom, phone call, etc.)
- Personal information like birthdays, anniversaries, kids' names, etc.

3. Send a "Next Steps" Email

After firming up your relationship in writing and gathering some helpful information, the last step in this process is to send your new client a thank-you email with the next steps for working together.

Keep it short and to the point – bullet points are great for this. Again, show your client right off the bat that working with you will make life easier, not add more to their busy schedule. Let your personality shine through and convey how excited you are to get started.

This onboarding system isn't set in stone. And as you move along in your journey as a VA, you'll likely work out a system that works even better for you and your style. Having a good system in place will give you confidence and reassure your client that they made a great choice in hiring you. Plus it confirms that you're a legit professional. You've totally got this.

On Contracts

Let's talk contracts for a minute. Do you really need one?

I think so, and here's why. The fact is that both you and your new client are entering into a trust relationship. They're trusting you to do what you say you'll do. And you're trusting them to communicate on a timely basis to get your work done and pay you. Unfortunately, there are flakey individuals out there on both sides of the equation.

While it's mostly unheard of, clients can either lag on payment or even seemingly disappear. It almost happened to me once. I was hired to write regularly scheduled blog posts for a startup. Their "marketing plan changed" not two months after we got started working together, and they were my largest client at the time.

Suddenly I had a hard time getting hold of them. And they still owed me $650 from my last invoice.

But we had a contract.

I was prepared to use one of my girlfriends, who's an attorney, to enforce it. But luckily a direct phone call (one the client actually answered) did the trick, and funds were wired to me immediately.

I did let them out of the rest of our contracted time, however. We were supposed to give one another 30 days' notice prior to cancelling the agreement. Since I had trouble getting paid on what I had recently delivered, there was no way I was about to write another month's worth of content and fight for payment.

So I let it go.

The bottom line is that things do happen, and a contract will protect you and your client.

It's important to point out that while drawing up a contract is a great idea, written agreements (like email) are also legally binding. So if you miss the contract boat for some reason, definitely have an email exchange in which you clarify the details of your working relationship and your client has indicated that they agree.

Contracts also help make things super clear right away. This safeguards against what we call scope creep, which is when your client adds new tasks that are not reflected in your pay.

Having your tasks clearly defined in writing helps you address this in a gentle, professional way. And it opens the conversation to increasing the scope of your role (and pay), which is a good thing.

Contract Components

Components of a contract may include:

- The tasks you'll be doing
- The number of hours you'll work per week (or day/month, this is up to you)
- Your rate of pay
- How you'll be paid
- When you'll be paid

You might also take this opportunity to identify details like what days and times you're available for contact, such as Monday through Friday from 9:00 a.m. to 5:00 p.m. CST. While the bullet points above are pretty standard and important to include, this is also an opportunity to flesh out how you want to run your business and be clear with clients upfront so there's no confusion.

If having a done-for-you client contract template would make things easier, you can purchase one here.[1]

Action Step

1. Write down your pre-interview game plan and some questions that you'd ask a potential client in an interview.

* * *

The process of landing that first client is a great experience. It's that feeling of *Yes! I'm totally doing this thing!* And as you go through the process a few times, you'll develop your own strategies for streamlining things according to your style and business. It gets easier each time.

Remember that your goal with interviewing is to explore whether this will be a good fit for both you and your potential client. Ask intelligent questions to get to know the business owner, what their business does, whom they serve, and how you can help them be more effective.

Once you've agreed to work together, you can step in confidently and get started as quickly as possible. Unless they have an established system of their own already, your client will appreciate your ability to streamline things and make the process run smoothly. You'll be confirming that they made the right decision to work with you.

Lastly, I recommend having a contract from the beginning. It clarifies your working relationship and avoids any awkward misunderstandings that could be detrimental to your long-term partnership. A contract also adds some security and helps promote trust for both you and your client. In the very slight chance that you'd need to pursue money owed to you, you'll have something to fall back on.

In the next chapter, we'll explore the fun part: getting paid!

9

COLLECT YOUR FIRST PAYCHECK

You've found that first client, worked out the details of your working relationship in writing, onboarded them like nobody's business, and have started working together.

And now comes an even more exciting part – getting paid. There are different ways to go about collecting payment from clients. But the bottom line is that you should use a method that makes it easy for them to pay you. That way you'll be sure to get paid on time, and your client will be grateful that you've made another part of this process as seamless as possible.

I'll go over a few of the more popular ways of collecting payment in this chapter. I'll also cover some basics that a proper business should have in place from an accounting perspective.

As a side note, while these business basics are important, they shouldn't be your primary focus right away – landing your first client should be.

You can and should begin pitching clients without these basics in place. Once you have a client or two under your belt, you can get your business more organized. This is definitely not a place to get stuck.

But getting things in order in the early days of your business will ultimately make things easier for you as you grow and add more clients.

First, let's dig into collecting your first paycheck. Ready?

Invoicing Clients

An invoice is simply the bill you'll send to your clients for the services you're providing. Invoices are also a way for both you and your client to keep track of your hours and pay, particularly when you're charging an hourly rate, as you most likely will be in the beginning.

Invoicing your client is your job. If you don't do it, you won't get paid.

It doesn't need to be a big deal. Here are some straightforward ways to go about it so you can ensure that you'll get paid as quickly as possible.

Create your own

You can create a simple invoice using a Word doc template or Excel spreadsheet. Of the options I'll share with you, this would be my least recommended one. Why? Because while it'll do the job, it's not convenient for your client. There's no button or link to click to easily pay you.

PayPal

PayPal is an easy way to get started with invoicing and receiving payments. It's a well-known platform that you can quickly and easily add some professional touches to, contributing to that legit business factor. You can even add a logo or profile photo and be ready to send an invoice within a couple of minutes!

You can upgrade a personal PayPal account to a business one for free. I recommend doing this after you secure your EIN – more on this soon. Upgrading adds some capabilities like automatic invoicing in the future. It's free to send invoices with PayPal, and there's a transaction fee of 2.9% + $0.30 (within the US) upon payment. Clients can pay with their PayPal balance or via their checking account (if it's linked to their PayPal account) or credit card.

QuickBooks

While I'd recommend PayPal as a quick and easy way to get started with invoicing, QuickBooks is also a great option at a low cost ($5 per month for the freelancer plan).

You may encounter clients who prefer not to use PayPal. QuickBooks offers a variety of payment methods, like credit card and bank transfer. You can also sync QuickBooks with other platforms like PayPal or Stripe, and you can even do your own bookkeeping with it.

Like PayPal, there's a 3% transaction fee with QuickBooks, unless you use a bank transfer. And really, these fees are just the cost of doing business. You can't avoid them, but if you feel you need to, you can inflate your fees slightly to cover the cost.

As a brand-new VA, Donna used QuickBooks to invoice her first client. She kept track of her hourly time with a tool called Evernote, then just cut and pasted the time into QuickBooks to send her invoices – "quick and easy," according to Donna.

Other invoicing options you might come across are FreshBooks ($15 per month for a basic plan), Xero ($9 per month), and Wave (free, but not very client-friendly in my opinion).

Like a lot of tools you'll encounter as you build your business, there are many options out there when it comes to invoicing. My personal favorite is QuickBooks. It's been around a while, is user-friendly, and doubles as your bookkeeping software.

Components of an Invoice

Using an invoicing platform like the ones we've just discussed will make things simple when it comes to what to include. You'll simply fill in the appropriate fields. But it's also good to know what you're filling in ahead of time.

1. **Invoice number** – This is adjustable, similar to being able to choose what number your checks start at. My default is usually 1001 rather than 001.
2. **Payment methods accepted** – This shows your client their options for how they can pay. Don't get hung up on transaction fees (3% is pretty standard), but instead make it a seamless process for your clients to choose which option they prefer so you can get paid faster. Most clients prefer not to pay via bank transfer in my experience.
3. **Payment terms** – I'd recommend choosing "due on receipt," but you can choose whatever works for you and your clients. Be sure it matches what you've outlined in your contract.
4. **Product/service and description fields** – This is where you'll choose or identify the service you're providing. You can describe what you're doing in the description field as well as assign a rate (flat, hourly, etc.).
5. **Message section** – This is where you can personalize your invoices, which is a nice touch. I like to thank clients for their business, but you can personalize this to fit your own style.
6. **Activity feed** – Some invoicing software (except PayPal) allows you to track if an invoice has been viewed. This is a great feature, as you'll be able to confirm that the client has received your invoice without having to ask them directly.
7. **Payment status** – Clients can access their invoices, which later become receipts when payment has been completed. It's likely that your invoicing software will show you at a glance which invoices have been paid and which are still outstanding on the main screen.

Final Thoughts on Invoicing

When you invoice your clients is completely up to you, either before you deliver services or after, or a combination of both. With your first client, you'll likely be sending an invoice after you've delivered services. The important part is to decide ahead of time and be clear with your client in your written agreement or contract so there is no confusion later.

As you move forward in your business, you'll develop a system that works for you, whether that means invoicing ahead of time, collecting a deposit before starting services, invoicing after work has been delivered, at certain benchmarks, or some combination of these.

For example, our team member Daryn bills after the first five business days when he takes on new WordPress website clients. Following that, he invoices at specific milestones – when certain tasks have been accomplished for the project he's working on.

The frequency of invoicing is also about what works for your business and income needs. Some VAs prefer to invoice weekly, every two weeks, or once a month. Again, just decide ahead of time and be clear with your client from the start.

You can decide to charge late fees and outline this in your initial contract, but you don't necessarily need to collect them. Be sure to clarify when payments are due. And be aware that identifying late fees and collecting them are two different things. Some clients will be very upset at the idea of paying them, but they're probably not your ideal client if they're paying you late anyway.

In my experience, the quicker a client pays their invoice, the more they value your work. This is also a good indicator of a successful working relationship.

For example, you can hear how appreciative and excited community member Samantha is about invoicing her very first client and getting paid promptly: *One month in with my first client, and I have to say how over the moon I am! She is simply amazing! She's incredibly talented, very nice and thoughtful, and I think she paid my invoice the second she received it.*

Working with clients you like and respect and who show they value your work by paying promptly makes a huge difference.

If for some reason a client hasn't paid you, don't continue to work for them. If it's a first-time offense, consider letting it slide once they've paid you. But if it's a repeated pattern, you may want to move on from the relationship.

Lastly, while rare, occasionally a client can go silent. While I hope this never happens to you, I also want you to feel confident and prepared as you launch out into the world of being a VA.

As I said earlier, the first way to handle this situation is to not do any more work for this client.

Next, a friendly but clear email check-in is a good way to start the conversation. Here's an example:

Hey [insert flakey client's name],

I just wanted to check in and confirm that you received the invoice I sent you on [date] for [services]? If you didn't for some reason, let me know, and I'll resend it.

I'm excited to continue working on [XYZ task(s)] as soon as payment has been made.

Talk soon,

[Your name]

If you still don't hear from a client after a friendly check-in/reminder, I recommend that you continue to email them. But also try reaching them other ways, like by phone and social media.

And depending on the amount you're owed, you'll have to decide how far you want to pursue things if a client continues to be unresponsive. Your options at that point would be to call it a wash and chalk it up to a learning experience, or hire an attorney to write them a strongly worded letter. You could also pursue using a collection agency if it seems worthwhile.

Now that we've covered the ins and outs of invoicing and getting paid, let's chat about some business basics.

Proper Business Basics

Let me reiterate: if you've been following along with the steps outlined in this book so far, you have everything you need to find your first clients, start working, and collect payment. In fact, you could run your business with your name and social security number forever. I did it this way for the first year of my business.

It's also good to know about some simple ways that you can formalize your business that will make things easier for you in the long run. So consider this information for when you've got a couple of clients under your belt and can take some time to work on your business.

Do *not* stop and get stuck here! Store this information away in your brain and revisit it later. And lastly, let me say that I'm not an accountant or lawyer.

While I do have a background as a financial advisor, I'm not giving you tax advice. When you're ready to expand your business, it's best to consult with a Certified Public Accountant (CPA) if you have questions.

Having said all that, let's move on. The list below isn't exhaustive but will be a good place to start when you're ready to move forward in the future.

Here are some components of a proper business:

1. An Official Business Name

As I've said, you can do business under your own name, and I actually recommend it. It's fun to come up with a creative name for your business. But branding your own name is a great way to go, too. You never know where this business will take you in the future. Building a brand around your name leaves the door open to exploring other avenues and opportunities in the world of online entrepreneurialism.

If you do decide to come up with a business name later, make sure it's easy to remember. And above all else, don't overthink it.

2. A Separate Mailing Address and Phone Number

You can run a VA business forever without these, depending on the types of clients you work with. There are some things that a physical address will come in handy for in the future though. For example, email campaigns legally require an address for newsletters and other communication. A post office (PO) box is sufficient.

And when it comes to a phone number, you can use a free option like Google Voice. Depending on the type of work you'll be doing, it's pretty rare that you'll need a phone for doing VA work, but it's not a bad idea to have a phone number available. Both of these are also a way of keeping your business separate from your personal life, and that's never a bad thing.

3. An Employer Identification Number (EIN)

An EIN is also known as a Federal Tax Identification Number and is used to identify you as a business. Having one will protect you from identity theft and puts another boundary between your personal life and your business. It also makes things easier when it comes to dealing with the IRS (in the US) and taxes. You'll need one for setting up a business checking account later.

When you're ready, this is one of the first things you'll want to take care of. You can easily apply for an EIN on the IRS's website. Don't use a third party, as it's free directly from the source. Just be sure to write it down because if you don't, it's a pain to track down the information later.

4. A Business Checking Account

It's really important that your business income does not go directly into your personal account. Why? Because the IRS frowns on this, and it makes for an accounting nightmare later.

Keeping your accounts separate right away also makes it easier to keep track of things like income and expenses for your business so you can stay organized. You'll be grateful for this when you have several clients and a growing business to keep up with.

Becca (another student of mine) also made a great point about why it's a good idea to keep your accounts separate: *I may have dragged my feet but I just got my EIN and I'm going to the bank today for a business account! I want to be able to see what I'm really making in this business and I know if I do it through my personal account that won't happen!*

While a separate bank account of any kind will do, it's not hard to set up a dedicated business account – often you can even do it over the phone or online. Do some research on the bank (or banks) you're thinking of working with and be sure to have the documentation they're requiring prepared ahead of time. It may be as simple as your social security number, EIN, and a minimum opening deposit, or they may require some additional documentation.

5. A System for Saving for Taxes

Lastly, aside from a business checking account to manage income and expenses, it's a good idea to have a business savings account for when tax season rolls around.

Remember, as a self-employed individual, you need to pay both the employer and the employee side of taxes plus your normal federal and state ones. I recommend setting aside 25% of your net (not gross) monthly income. Transfer this to your separate business savings account and forget about it.

It's a good idea to get some input from a CPA on this topic as your business grows. That way you'll be prepared and can position yourself monthly to avoid any surprises come tax time.

While taxes vary from state to state (and country to country), VA and community member Marcie has some helpful general insight into filing taxes as a freelancer. Remember to consult with your CPA about these items at tax time.

Hey everyone! I just spent several hours with a CPA doing taxes so wanted to share some info with you for your VA businesses.

Things I deducted for my business (which I am sure is not all of them but can get you started):

- *Training – Any training, including courses*
- *Social media scheduling tools – If you pay for them for your own biz or for clients*
- *Website fees and construction if you hired help*
- *Office supplies – Some that I had were a new printer, computer, plastic shield for under my computer chair, paper, ink cartridges, etc.*
- *The square footage of my office, a room designated just for my business, compared to the total footage of my entire home to establish a percentage*
- *You will also need to have a yearly total of what you paid for:*
- *Mortgage*
- *House insurance*
- *House taxes*
- *Electricity*
- *Any other household utilities*

You can also deduct a percentage of your home phone, cell phone, and internet based on how much you use each for your business.

I hope this helps as some of you are just starting your business – keep your receipts and you'll be ahead of the game when tax season comes next year!

Action Steps

1. Decide how you're going to invoice your first client and set it up now.
2. Take some time to get familiar with what you're using and send yourself a test invoice.

* * *

While some of what I've covered in this chapter might not be the most exciting stuff, in a way it is. There's something magical about getting that first payment from a client, and it's another milestone in your journey that says you're officially a VA!

Prepare ahead of time and decide how you'll collect your first paycheck – that way you'll be ready when the time comes. Remember to make things as easy and seamless as possible for your client. That way you'll not only get paid faster, but you'll also continue your theme of making their lives easier, not more complicated.

Focus on landing that first client and getting paid for now, but also keep in mind that you're building a legitimate business. If you treat it like a hobby, it will pay you like one. But if you really own it, the sky's the limit! Don't worry about some of the in-depth setup for now, but do be aware of some of the simple first steps you can take to further legitimize your business in the future.

Are you ready for the last step? It's time to take a glance into the future and explore how to scale your thriving business.

10

SCALE YOUR BUSINESS

You are now at the last step in the journey of getting started as a VA. Congratulations! The fact that you've made it this far shows that you're willing to spend some time investing in your future by educating yourself.

That's a characteristic that will take you far no matter what you decide to pursue in life.

And when it comes to creating a side- or full-time income offering services online, you now have everything you need to land your first client. Take a minute to check in with yourself about that. How are you feeling? Excited? Nervous? Both?

Now that you have a clear vision of the incredible opportunity there is for you as a VA, and have a systematic approach to getting started, you're hopefully feeling excited. Being a little nervous is normal. It just means you're onto something big here.

In this chapter I'm going to cover what it means to scale your business and where you go from here. Before we get into that, let's do a brief review of the last eight steps we covered.

If you haven't already, now is a great time to download your companion workbook which will help you implement the action steps listed throughout this book. You can find it at:

https://horkeyhandbook.com/book-bonus/

Step 1: Take Inventory of Your Skills

We covered what kinds of traits make you a great VA and how to think about this from the perspective of a business owner who is looking for a VA to trust with the inner workings of their business. This will give you a good understanding of the best traits you can bring to the table.

We also discussed how to take inventory of your existing skills – whether they're obvious or not so obvious. Remember that virtually everyone has a skill that can be turned into a service to offer the marketplace. That includes you.

Lastly, we spent some time setting some goals for today and your long-term future. Create goals that are S.M.A.R.T (specific, measurable, actionable, results-oriented, and time-sensitive), and you'll be well on your way to achieving them.

Action Step 1: Take a few minutes and review the six traits below to see how you fare.

- Organized
- Reliable
- Positive attitude
- Takes initiative
- Communicates well
- Open to learning new things

Action Step 2: Set a timer for 15 minutes and write down three to five skills you currently have:

1._____

2. _____

3. _____

4. _____

5. _____

Action Step 3: Take a minute to envision where you'd like to be in the next:

Year: _____

Three years: _____

Five years: _____

If this intimidates you, feel free to focus on shorter timelines like 30, 90, and 180 days.

Step 2: Choose Your First Service Offering

In this step, we covered how to take those skills and turn them into a service offering. Remember, you're going to find a client much quicker if you're clear on what you're offering versus being willing to do anything for anyone. The latter is not a big confidence-builder for a business owner and makes you the equivalent of a virtual handyman.

We explored the various categories of services, and I encouraged you to spend time with these and figure out what resonates the most with you. Remember, this isn't set in stone. It's just a place to get started for now. You can also review the list of "150+ Services You Can Offer as a Virtual Assistant" to give you an idea of the possibilities out there.

You don't need to limit yourself to this list, by the way. There's something for everyone when it comes to offering services online.

Action Step 1: It's time to choose your primary service offering(s).

Read through the 150+ Services pdf. [1]

Action Step 2: Choose one to two services that you currently know how to do that you can offer to prospective clients.

Service offering #1: _____

Service offering #2: _____

Action Step 3: Locate another two to three services that you are interested in learning more about.

Alternate service offering #1: _____

Alternate service offering #2: _____

Alternate service offering #3: _____

Step 3: Set Your Rates

So how much can you make as a VA? We covered what the going rates are for Virtual Assistants as well as the different ways you can get paid. As you're just starting out, you will likely charge an hourly rate, which makes things easy for you and your new client.

Later on, you can shift gears and start charging retainer rates. For now, though, use the guidelines in this step to figure out what hourly rate makes the most sense for you. Keep in mind that this is just a starting place.

Raise your rates appropriately with each new client as you gain more experience and add skills to your virtual tool belt. And remember, as you specialize your services and hone in on a target market, the sky's the limit when it comes to your income.

Action Step: Using the calculations provided in this step, decide on the hourly rate you'd like to start with.

Step 4: Prepare Your Online Presence

Now that you have some of the basics of your business in place, you'll need somewhere to send potential clients. It's time to set up your virtual storefront. You can do this with a resume tailored to your VA-specific skills and experiences, a social media profile (or profiles) optimized for your business, or a Hire Me page on your website if you already have one.

This is a fun step, as you start sharing publicly what you're up to with your new, exciting adventure as a VA. Some new VAs subconsciously sabotage themselves by getting stuck here and overthinking things. It's a subtle way of procrastinating on getting out there and finding clients.

My suggestion would be to start with an optimized social media profile and go from there. As with all of these steps, you can (and should) go back and build out the foundation of your business after you've landed that first client or three.

Action Step: Choose one of the three ways and build out your online presence.

Step 5: Sourcing Prospects to Pitch

So now that you're all set to go and find your first client, where should you look? The source of your first paying gig may be a lot closer than you think, and you definitely don't want to underestimate your immediate network or natural market.

Head into sourcing clients with the right mindset. Your confidence and positive attitude will make all the difference when you're talking with potential clients.

Take inventory of who in your immediate network might need help or who might know someone who needs help. You can also source clients on social media and/or by doing some research on the internet. All three of these have proven to be effective sources of first clients for many VAs. I see it all the time.

Action Step: Make a list of 10 potential clients to reach out to.

Step 6: Send Your First Few Pitches

Alright, you have a list of potential dream clients to reach out to. Now what? There are some "pitching best practices" to include when you pitch your services to a business owner. Be sure to review these and check the boxes when you're sending those first few pitches. And remember that pitching will get easier and easier with time and practice.

You may hear some "nos" before you hear a "yes," but pitching tends to have a cumulative effect. The more you do it, the more momentum you build. The seeds you may have sown days, weeks, or even months prior do yield a harvest. Until you have a full client roster, remember that pitching is the lifeblood of your business and that you should be spending the time you have available doing it.

Action Step: Send two pitches each day, Monday through Friday.

Step 7: Land Your First Client

As there can be so much effort that goes into finding that first client, when you actually hear a "yes, let's talk," it can be a shock. Know that it's coming and prepare yourself so that when it does, you'll be able to move forward like the poised professional you are.

In the online business world, interviews look a bit different and can be a fun opportunity to connect with another business owner. They don't need to be scary or anxiety-inducing with the right mindset heading in.

And once you get that "yes, let's do this" (from both of you), you'll be ready to onboard your new client like a pro. This will set the tone for your assistance right off the bat and reassure your new client that they've made the right choice.

Lastly, you'll also want to start things off the right way by getting the important details in writing, like how and when you'll be paid and how much. While an email exchange is legally sufficient, it's a good idea to get a signed contract from a client to make things crystal clear in your working relationship from the beginning.

Action Step 1: Write down your pre-interview game plan and some questions that you'd ask a potential client in an interview.

Action Step 2: In need of a customizable contract template? You can grab one very reasonably here.[2]

Step 8: Collect Your First Paycheck

You've arrived! You've started working with a client, and it's time to get paid. Invoicing can be a simple process, and there are several ways to go about it. I've offered a few of the easiest and more popular options. But the goal is to make things as seamless as possible for your client so you can get paid quickly.

In this step, we also took a look at the basic aspects of a proper business from an accounting perspective. Don't spend much time with these now. But you'll want to circle back around and tend to some of these basics after you have a few clients under your belt. Doing so will keep you organized for the future when you're spending the majority of your time doing client work, and you'll be glad you did!

Action Step: Decide how you're going to invoice your first client and set it up now. Take some time to get familiar with the program you're using and send yourself a test invoice.

Now that we've had a refresher, let's take a look at what's next for you.

Scaling Your Business: What Does It Mean?

Remember, my goal for you with this book and these actionable steps is to land your first client as quickly as possible. But what's next for you?

This is a good time to circle back to the goals you set for yourself in Step One and give this some thought. Scaling your business means taking it to the next level. Depending on your ultimate goal(s), this can be an ongoing process of watching your business grow to places you never thought possible or perhaps seeing it get to a place that's just right for you and your needs or desires.

My recent venture as a college professor is a great example of this. If you had told me back in 2014 that I'd be asked to develop a university program to teach people the skills of running a service-based business, I'm not sure I would have believed you.

But it's the real deal, and it's just one amazing turn in the road of my online journey these last several years. While it's been a lot of hard work and at times challenging, I've loved seeing my business evolve and develop. And I've loved seeing how it's impacted other people even more.

Back to you and your journey...

After you've worked through these steps and landed your first client, scaling your business should involve finding as many new clients as you can until your roster is full. Depending on your long-term goals, this can evolve a few different ways.

Part-Time

If you're looking to create a side-hustle income and do this part-time, you'll know when you're at capacity for what you can manage time-wise. Your next step would be to either charge your existing clients more, increase the caliber of new clients and subsequently raise your rates, or add skills and services that you can upgrade your work (and rates) with. The goal is to make the most income with the time you have available.

Full-Time

If your goal is to build a full-time VA business, then your "benchmarks" are a full client roster as well as bringing in the income that will make this work for you. Keep in mind that "full-time" doesn't necessarily mean full-time hours but can be defined strictly by the income you're bringing in. Scaling would be a similar scenario as a part-time VA – maximizing the time you have available by honing your skills and raising your rates.

And from there? In either case, part-time or full-time, the sky's the limit. Once you're at capacity with your client roster, you may decide to start working with other VAs by outsourcing tasks and pursuing an agency model.

For example, Mallory, a past student and friend, moved to an agency model just 10 months after launching her VA business. She saw the opportunity to not only scale her business beyond the time she had available in her schedule, but to be able to offer a wider variety of services to a larger variety of clients. Mallory also considers supporting other women working from home a huge win for her business.

You may also decide to shift gears and explore the online business world even more. Getting started as a VA is the best way to break in online and learn how things work in the virtual marketing landscape. You might decide to take the skills you've learned and apply them to another entrepreneurial vision one day, like me.

This journey could open incredible doors for you if you keep the right mindset and focus. For now, set your sights on scaling your VA business to the next level, and that means filling your client roster.

We've covered everything you need to know to land that first client or two. Here are some additional things to consider when scaling your business further:

- Getting clear on your positioning statement – what do you do and whom do you do it for?
- Figuring out and getting to know your target market
- Building a VA website
- Exploring higher-quality and more diverse lead sources
- Increasing your pitching game
- Offering package rates

- Honing the nuances of working with clients to become a higher-quality VA
- Equipping yourself with tools and resources that make your clients' lives (and yours) easier
- Niching down and specializing your services.

Pay particular attention to that last bullet point. It's number one when it comes to landing quality clients, charging more for your services, and scaling your business.

11

CONCLUSION

Well, if you've made it this far, then chances are good that you're ready to build a successful, sustainable VA business, one that provides:

- Flexibility
- Opportunities to use current skills and learn new ones
- Hours that suit you
- The chance to work with some amazing clients
- Unlimited earning potential

But it's not enough to read a great book. You have to take action. If you're ready to continue your journey (and fill your client roster), you could consider enrolling in #FullyBookedVaSystem,[1] our online VA Program. We go way more in-depth on the subjects and steps in this book and invite you to join our VA Leads Community when you do. That's where we dole out high-quality client lead introductions, offer regular and live office hours (with me!), plus additional training and mentorship.

If you haven't yet downloaded the workbook, head over to:

https://horkeyhandbook.com/book-bonus/

It contains all of the action steps you need to create a business you love. As we've covered here, the workbook will also help you get clear on the kinds of clients you want to serve and the services you can offer them.

Just know that you're in exactly the right place at exactly the right time to make your goals and dreams for life on your terms a reality. Building a legitimate business for yourself is by no means a get-rich-quick model. But with the right information, support, and focus, it's one that works for the long term.

Why not YOU, why not NOW?

If you enjoyed this book, check out the other titles in the Make Money From Home series at sallyannmiller.com/books

NOTES

1. Introduction

1. https://www.entrepreneur.com/article/238352
2. https://www.forbes.com/sites/elainepofeldt/2017/10/17/are-we-ready-for-a-workforce-that-is-50-freelance/#560d5c883f82
3. http://fullybookedva.com/join

3. Choose Your First Service Offering

1. https://drive.google.com/file/d/1bt5Tsjz_XZ4GR4__GGiZ3iufMNtG1bCS/view
2. https://drive.google.com/file/d/1bt5Tsjz_XZ4GR4__GGiZ3iufMNtG1bCS/view

5. Prepare Your Online Presence

1. http://fullybookedva.com/join

8. Land Your First Client

1. https://horkeyhandbook.samcart.com/products/client-contract

10. Scale Your Business

1. https://drive.google.com/file/d/1bt5Tsjz_XZ4GR4__GGiZ3iufMNtG1bCS/view
2. https://horkeyhandbook.samcart.com/products/client-contract

11. Conclusion

1. http://fullybookedva.com/join

ABOUT GINA HORKEY

Gina Horkey is a married millennial mama to two precocious kiddos from Minnesota.

In addition to PodcastProductionSchool.com, she's also the founder of several websites: HorkeyHandBook.com, UploadUniversity.com, KidsVsBikini.com and GinaHorkey.com.

Gina has specialized in helping everyday folks learn hard digital marketing skills to launch their own service-based businesses online, working from the comfort of their own home (or anywhere!) since 2014.

Her background includes making a living as a professional writer, an online business marketing consultant and a decade of experience in the financial services industry.

EXCERPT: MAKE MONEY AS A FREELANCE WRITER

GINA HORKEY & SALLY MILLER

And suddenly you know: it's time to start something new and trust the magic of beginnings.

— Meister Eckhart

When you begin an adventure, you're filled with hope. The future holds promise. Your excitement gives you momentum. You're ready to take on the world. This is the magic of a new beginning.

You picked up this book because you're searching for a beginning. You dream about earning a living as a writer.

Perhaps you need a flexible career that allows you to stay home with your kids. Or you want to earn money as you travel the world. Maybe you long to quit your nine to five job.

Whatever your reasons, you want to make money doing something you love—writing.

Everyone's journey is different. It's possible you've always enjoyed writing, yet never thought you could make money from your passion.

Or perhaps you're like me. You discovered a love for writing by accident.

I enjoyed writing as a kid, but the school system in the U.K. forces students to specialize early. I picked the sciences. And soon my time was taken up with experiments, equations, and methods. There was no space left for writing.

When I graduated, I followed a career in Information Technology, my childhood love for writing forgotten.

Then something happened. I was home with a new baby, searching for ways to occupy my mind while earning some money. I attended an online conference for writers and came away inspired.

Four months later, I'd written and published my first book. Then I wrote another one. I enjoyed writing so much, I started to freelance. I found clients who were willing to pay me to write.

At last, I'd discovered a way to pay the bills while doing something I loved.

Freelance Writing Challenges

My journey wasn't simple. I encountered many challenges along the way. Some of these I overcame and some I learned to live with.

As you contemplate starting a career as a freelance writer, you probably share some of my concerns.

You don't know how to get started or how much to charge.

You're afraid of failing. You don't want to tell friends and family that you followed your dreams for nothing.

You're scared of rejection. You ask yourself, what if you can't find clients? What if your clients hate your work?

I've faced all these fears and more. But I've learned that if you want something enough, you can get past your doubts.

In the next chapter, I discuss the most common concerns. I share stories from other freelance writers who've done exactly what you hope to do. All of them faced their fears and started freelance writing careers.

How to Start Your Freelance Writing Business

I learned everything I needed to know from my co-author, Gina Horkey.

I first met Gina when I took her Freelance Writing Course. I was impressed by how quickly she'd found success in her career. Just six months after starting, Gina was earning over $4,000 per month.

I decided that I would learn from Gina and try freelance writing for myself. I took her course and followed the process she taught. It's the same system we describe in this book.

In my third month, I earned $1,100 while staying home with two young children. I had little free time for writing. Between diapers and naps, I could barely spare an hour per day for my new business.

I can't predict how long it will take you to earn your first $1,000. It depends on how much time you commit to the process. But what I *do* know is this—if I can do it, so can you.

This book is not for experienced writers who are further along in their career. It's also not for people who aren't prepared to follow the steps and do the work.

However, if you're one hundred percent committed to starting a freelance writing business, then this book *is* for you.

The Seven Steps to Start Your Freelance Business

So, how does this book work?

We've organized it into a series of sequential steps. We've done this so that you know exactly what to do and when to do it.

Gina wrote the middle chapters and I wrote the opening and closing chapters. You'll notice a change of writing style from one chapter to the next. We're two different people with very different styles. We think that's a good thing, since you get to benefit from both of our experiences!

The steps to start your freelance writing business are:

> Step 1: Pick your writing niche(s)

> Step 2: Gather writing samples

> Step 3: Create a portfolio

> Step 4: Source jobs

> Step 5: Start pitching

> Step 6: Land your first client

> Step 7: Earn your first $1,000

In each chapter, we explain what to do and how to do it. We include concrete action items for you to follow. If you consistently take action, then you will see results. It may take 30 days or it may take 90 days. But you will earn $1,000 as a freelance writer.

There is demand for your writing skills. According to the U.S. Bureau of Labor Statistics, in 2015 the median wage for freelance writers was $60,250. The top 10 percent earned over $114,530. Given that one in four writers work part-time, this is a healthy living for someone doing work that they love.

Now it's your turn. Read the next chapter and face your fears. Then take the first step to start your freelance writing business.

Remember, you're not alone. We and hundreds of other writers have already taken these steps and are living our dream. Don't wait until tomorrow. Start today.

Keep Reading Make Money As A Freelance Writer – available in online bookstores now!

Manufactured by Amazon.ca
Bolton, ON